TASTY
Crochet

A Pantry Full of Patterns for 33 Yummy Treats

Rose Langlitz

NORTH LIGHT BOOKS

Cincinnati, Ohio

www.mycraftivity.com

13 12 11 10 09   5 4 3 2 1

Distributed in Canada by Fraser Direct
100 Armstrong Avenue
Georgetown, ON, Canada L7G 5S4
Tel: (905) 877-4411

Distributed in the U.K. and Europe by David & Charles
Brunel House, Newton Abbot, Devon, TQ12 4PU, England
Tel: (+44) 1626 323200, Fax: (+44) 1626 323319
E-mail: postmaster@davidandcharles.co.uk

Distributed in Australia by Capricorn Link
P.O. Box 704, S. Windsor, NSW 2756 Australia
Tel: (02) 4577-3555

Library of Congress Cataloging-in-Publication Data

Langlitz, Rose.
  Tasty crochet : a pantry full of patterns for 33 yummy treats / Rose Langlitz. -- 1st ed.
       p. cm.
  Includes index.
  ISBN-13: 978-1-60061-312-8 (pbk. : alk. paper)
  ISBN-10: 1-60061-312-8 (pbk. : alk. paper)
 1. Crocheting--Patterns. 2. Food in art. I. Title.
  TT825.L363 2009
  746.43'4041--dc22
                          2008036003

Please note: The patterns in this book are intended for the creation of play food, and items created should not be considered as chewable toys for pets or children.

Editor: Tonia Davenport
Designer: Corrie Schaffeld
Production Coordinator: Greg Nock
Photographer: Richard Deliantoni
Photo Stylist: Lauren Emmerling

fw
F+W PUBLICATIONS, INC.

 Acknowledgments

I'd like to thank everyone who made this book possible, most especially Tonia Davenport, Editor Extraordinaire. I appreciate her patience and encouragement, and she has been a pleasure to work with.

To my ever supportive husband, who never complains when he has to move yarn in order to sit down.

Rose Langlitz

Rose Langlitz lives in Cincinnati, Ohio, with her handsome hubby and four slightly mischievous children. In her spare time, Rose enjoys crocheting, daydreaming about her yarn stash, and long walks on the beach.

Contents

Know Your Way Around the Kitchen 7

🍗 Dinner 73

🍦 Dessert 101

Know Your Way Around the Kitchen

Need a little fiber in your diet?

The patterns in this book are simple and quick to make. You can make an apple in just one sitting, or you can spend a day and cook up the entire breakfast menu. Even if you are a beginning crocheter, you'll find that making a slice of bread is easy as pie!

You will notice that all of my patterns call for wool, cotton, or blended yarns. Wool has a natural stretch that makes it ideal for this type of structural crochet, but any yarns in the right weights and colors can be substituted.

If you take a peek ahead, you'll see that I don't have the gauge listed for any projects. This is because most of the pieces in this book are small enough that by the time you have a 4″ x 4″ (10cm x 10cm) swatch made, you have already spent nearly as much time as you would have making, say, a carrot. I trust that if your pancake comes out the size of a dinner plate, you'll realize that you may need to use a smaller hook and tighten up your stitches!

I hope you'll have lots and lots of fun whipping up the patterns in this book, and I hope that they inspire you to expand your crochet palette in new and exciting ways!

Breakfast

Everyone knows that this first meal of the day can be the most important. Eating breakfast improves concentration, helps you maintain a healthy weight and gives you the ability to fly. Well, maybe not that last part, but the point is that it's really good for you. Celebrate your love for breakfast with a big plate of fried eggs, bacon and a little toast on the side. Pressed for time? Make an on-the-go meal of a bagel half or a yummy toaster pastry. You could even try to set a record for the tallest stack of pancakes in the world. No matter what you decide to have for breakfast, have fun with it and wake me up when it's ready.

Ah . . . the smell of bacon in the morning. When it's done sizzling, block your bacon flat if you'd like, or leave it with that natural crochet ripple. Recipe Idea: Pair the bacon with the bread (page 49), lettuce (page 59) and tomato (page 59) to create a BLT.

Bacon

Ingredients

1 skein Lion Brand Wool-Ease (wool/acrylic/polyester blend, 197 yds [179m] per 85g skein) in color Chestnut Heather

1 skein Lion Brand Fisherman's Wool (wool, 465 yds [425m] per 227g skein) in color Natural

(or comparable worsted weight yarns)

US G / 4.0mm hook

With Chestnut Heather, ch 22.

Row 1 (RS): *Sc in first two ch, dec over next two ch, sc in next two ch, 2 sc in next ch; rep from * two more times. Ch 1, turn—21 sc.

Row 2: Sc in each sc across. Change to Natural. Ch 1, turn.

Row 3: Rep Row 1. Change to Chestnut Heather. Ch 1, turn.

Row 4: Rep Row 2.

Row 5: Rep Row 1. Change to Natural. Ch 1, turn.

Row 6: Rep Row 2. Change to Chestnut Heather. Ch 1, turn.

Row 7: Rep Row 1.

Fasten off, weave in ends.

Bring your bagel to the table as is, or add some strawberry cream cheese. Substitute pink-colored wool and crochet as for the white portion, only omit the last round and sew to the top of your bagel. Or, make two halves of the camel-colored sections and stitch them together to make a fluffy doughnut!

Bagel Half

Ingredients

1 skein Patons Classic Wool (wool, 223 yds [203m] per 100g skein) in color Winter White

1 skein Patons Classic Wool (wool, 223 yds [203m] per 100g skein) in color Camel

(or comparable worsted weight yarns)

US G / 4.0mm hook

stitch marker

yarn needle

polyester fiberfill for stuffing

 NOTES:

- This pattern is worked in continuous rnds. Please be sure to place a marker in the first stitch of rnd.
- The first piece of this pattern will naturally curl as you crochet. Because of the curling, the inside (WS) of the bagel half will be facing you as you work.

With Camel, ch 10. Sl st to first ch to form a ring.

Rnd 1 (WS): Sc in same ch as join and in each ch around—10 sc.

Rnd 2: Sc in first sc, 2 sc in next sc, [sc in next sc, 2 sc in next sc] four times—15 sc.

Rnd 3: Sc in first sc and in each sc around.

Rnd 4: Sc in first sc and in next sc, 2 sc in next sc, [sc in each of the next two sc, 2 sc in next sc] four times—20 sc.

Rnd 5: Sc in first sc, 2 sc in next sc, [sc in next sc, 2 sc in next sc] nine times—30 sc.

Rnd 6: Sc in first sc and in each sc around.

Rnd 7: Sc in first sc, 2 sc in next sc, [sc in next sc, 2 sc in next sc] fourteen times—45 sc.

Rnd 8: Sc in first sc and in each sc around.

Rnd 9: Sc in first sc and in next sc, 2 sc in next sc, [sc in each of the next two sc, 2 sc in next sc] fourteen times—60 sc.

Rnd 10: Sc in first sc and in each sc around.

Rnds 11–13: Rep Rnd 10.

Fasten off, leaving a long tail for sewing.

With Winter White, ch 10. Sl st to first ch to form a ring.

Rnd 1 (RS): Sc in same ch as join and in each ch around—10 sc.

Rnd 2: Work 2 sc in first sc and in each sc around—20 sc.

Rnd 3: Sc in first sc, 2 sc in next sc, [sc in next sc, 2 sc in next sc] nine times—30 sc.

Rnd 4: Sc in first sc and in next sc, 2 sc in next sc, [sc in each of the next two sc, 2 sc in next sc] nine times—40 sc.

Rnd 5: Sc in first sc and in each of the next two sc, 2 sc in next sc, [sc in each of the next three sc, 2 sc in next sc] nine times—50 sc.

Rnd 6: Sc in first sc and in each of the next three sc, 2 sc in next sc, [sc in each of the next four sc, 2 sc in next sc] nine times—60 sc.

Fasten off, leaving a long tail for sewing.

Finishing: With RS facing out, align the two pieces tog. First, seam the center rounds, taking care to match up the sts. Then, seam the outside edges, working through both loops of the sts on the white piece and the inner loop of the sts of the brown piece. Stuff with fiberfill when small gap remains, complete seam. Fasten off and weave in ends.

Whether you prefer them poached or fried, two eggs in the morning will satisfy you for hours. Serve with a couple of toast triangles (page 23) and perhaps some bacon (page 11), and you're sure to start your day off right. Salt and pepper to taste.

Fried Egg

Ingredients

1 skein Patons Classic Wool (wool, 223 yds [203m] per 100g skein) in color Winter White

1 skein Lion Brand Lion Wool (wool, 158 yds [144m] per 85g skein) in color Goldenrod

(or comparable worsted weight yarns)

US G / 4.0mm hook

stitch marker

yarn needle

❋ NOTE:

- This pattern is worked in continuous rnds. Please be sure to place a marker in the first stitch of rnd.

Egg White

With Winter White, ch 2.

Rnd 1 (RS): Work 8 sc in second ch from hook—8 sc.

Rnd 2: Work 2 sc in each sc around—16 sc.

Rnd 3: [Sc in sc, 2 sc in next sc] three times, hdc in next sc, 2 hdc in next sc, [dc in next sc, 2 dc in next sc] two times, hdc in next sc, 2 hdc in next sc, sc in next sc, 2 sc in next sc—24 sts.

Rnd 4: [Sc in next two sts, 2 sc in next st] two times, [hdc in next two sts, 2 hdc in next st] two times, [dc in next two sts, 2 dc in next st] two times, hdc in next two sts, 2 hdc in next st, sc in next two sts, 2 sc in next st—32 sts.

Rnd 5: [Sc in three sts, 2 sc in next st] three times, hdc in three sts, 2 hdc in next st, [dc in three sts, 2 dc in next st] two times, hdc in three sts, 2 hdc in next st, sc in three sts, 2 sc in next st—40 sts.

Rnd 6: [Sc in three sts, 2 sc in next st] four times, hdc in three sts, 2 hdc in next st, [dc in three sts, 2 dc in next st] two times, hdc in three sts, 2 hdc in next st, [sc in three sts, 2 sc in next st] two times—50 sts.

Fasten off, weave in ends.

Yolk

With Goldenrod, ch 2.

Rnd 1 (RS): Work 6 sc in second ch from hook—6 sc.

Rnd 2: Work 2 sc in each sc around—12 sc.

Rnd 3: [Sc in sc, 2 sc in next sc] around—18 sc.

Rnd 4: Sc around.

Fasten off, leaving a long tail for sewing.

 Finishing: Center the yolk over the beg round of the egg white. Using the tail of the yolk and yarn needle, stitch around the yolk, securing it to the white. Fasten off, weave in ends.

Egg in the Shell

Ingredients

1 skein Patons Classic Wool (wool, 223 yds [203m] per 100g skein) in color Winter White

US G / 4.0mm Hook

Yarn needle

Top Half

With Winter White, ch 2.

Rnd 1 (RS): Work 8 sc in second ch from hook. Join with a sl st to first sc, ch 1—8 sc.

Rnd 2: Sc in same st as join, 2 sc in next sc, [sc in next sc, 2 sc in next sc] three times. Join with sl st to first sc, ch 1—12 sc.

Rnd 3: Sc in same st as join and in next sc, 2 sc in next sc, [sc in each of the next two sc, 2 sc in next sc] three times. Join with sl st to first sc, ch 1—16 sc.

Rnd 4: Sc in same st as join and in each of the next two sc, 2 sc in next sc, [sc in each of the next three sc, 2 sc in next sc] three times. Join with sl st to first sc, ch 1—20 sc.

Rnd 5: Sc in same st as join and in each of the next two sc, 2 sc in next sc, [sc in each of the next three sc, 2 sc in next sc] four times. Join with sl st to first sc, ch 1—25 sc.

Rnd 6: Sc in same st as join and in each of the next 24 sc. Join with sl st to first sc, ch 1.

Rnds 7-9: Rep Rnd 6. Do not work ch 1 at the end of Rnd 9. Fasten off, weave in ends.

Bottom Half

With Winter White, ch 2.

Rnd 1 (RS): Work 10 sc in second ch from hook. Join with a sl st to first sc, ch 1—10 sc.

Rnd 2: Sc in same st as join, 2 sc in next sc, [sc in next sc, 2 sc in next sc] four times. Join with sl st to first sc, ch 1—15 sc.

Rnd 3: Sc in same st as join and in next sc, 2 sc in next sc, [sc in each of the next two sc, 2 sc in next sc] four times. Join with sl st to first sc, ch 1—20 sc.

Rnd 4: Sc in same st as join and in each of the next two sc, 2 sc in next sc, [sc in each of the next three sc, 2 sc in next sc] four times. Join with sl st to first sc, ch 1—25 sc.

Rnd 5: Sc in same st as join and in each of the next 24 sc. Join with sl st to first sc, ch 1.

Rnds 6-9: Rep Rnd 5. Do not work ch 1 at the end of Rnd 9. Fasten off, leaving a long tail for sewing.

❋ **Finishing:** Match up sts on the two halves of the eggshell. Whipstitch the two halves tog about halfway across, leaving ample room to tuck the fried egg inside. Fasten off, weave in ends.

Call them flapjacks, hotcakes, or whatever you'd like; pancakes are a delicious breakfast tradition. Add strawberries (page 129) and a nice dollop of whipped cream (page128) for a real breakfast treat. Make just a couple, or pile them high!

Pancake

 NOTE:

• This pattern is worked in continuous rnds. Please be sure to place a marker in the first stitch of rnd.

Make two:

With Camel, ch 2.

Rnd 1 (RS): Work 8 sc in second ch from hook—8 sc.

Rnd 2: Work 2 sc in each sc around—16 sc.

Rnd 3: [Sc in sc, 2 sc in next sc] eight times—24 sc.

Rnd 4: [Sc in next two sc, 2 sc in next sc] eight times—32 sc.

Rnd 5: [Sc in next three sc, 2 sc in next sc] eight times—40 sc.

Rnd 6: [Sc in next four sc, 2 sc in next sc] eight times—48 sc.

Rnd 7: [Sc in next five sc, 2 sc in next sc] eight times—56 sc.

Rnd 8: [Sc in next six sc, 2 sc in next sc] eight times—64 sc.

Rnd 9: Sc in each sc around.

Fasten off, weave in ends.

 Finishing: Pin the two circles with WS tog. Using Winter White yarn, crochet through both pieces all the way around. Fasten off, weave in ends.

Block flat.

Ingredients

1 skein Patons Classic Wool (wool, 223 yds [203m] per 100g skein) in color Camel

1 skein Patons Classic Wool (wool, 223 yds [203m] per 100g skein) in color Winter White

(or comparable worsted weight yarns)

US G / 4.0mm hook

yarn needle

Breakfast can't be complete without a little toast, and who doesn't prefer their toast cut on the diagonal? Use the yarn colors listed below, or vary with a darker shade for wheat. If you're feeling adventurous, crochet up a little yellow square for a yummy pat of butter.

Toast Triangle

Ingredients

1 skein Patons Classic Wool (wool, 223 yds [203m] per 100g skein) in color Winter White

1 skein Patons Classic Wool (wool, 223 yds [203m] per 100g skein) in color Camel

(or comparable worsted weight yarns)

US G / 4.0mm hook

yarn needle

With Winter White, ch 18.

Row 1 (RS): Sc in second ch from hook and in each ch across. Ch 1, turn—17 sc.

Row 2: Sc in each sc across. Ch 1, turn.

Rows 3–18: Rep Row 2.

Fasten off. With Camel and RS facing, sc all the way around the piece, working 2 sc in each corner. Fasten off, weave in ends.

 Finishing: Fold the piece in half diagonally to form a triangle. Using a long strand of Camel and yarn needle, match up the sts and sew through the edges to secure tog. Fasten off, weave in ends. Block flat.

Nothing beats a sweet, warm toaster pastry when you're in a hurry. Have fun with this pattern and mix it up a little bit—make some white icing with chocolate sprinkles, or have a chocolate toaster pastry with blueberry icing. The sky's the limit!

Toaster Pastry

Ingredients

1 skein Patons Classic Wool (wool, 223 yds [203m] per 100g skein) in color Camel

1 skein Patons Classic Wool (wool, 223 yds [203m] per 100g skein) in color Petal Pink

1 skein Patons Classic Wool (wool, 223 yds [203m] per 100g skein) in color Winter White

(or comparable worsted weight yarns)

US G / 4.0mm hook

yarn needle

Pastry (Make two):

With Camel yarn, ch 17.

Row 1 (RS): Sc in second ch from hook and in each ch across. Ch 1, turn—16 sc.

Row 2: Sc in first sc and in each sc across. Ch 1, turn.

Rows 3-24: Rep Row 2.

Fasten off, weave in ends.

Pin the two pieces with WS tog. Starting on a short side, crochet through both pieces all the way around, working 3 sc in each corner.

Fasten off, weave in ends.

Icing

With Petal Pink, ch 13.

Row 1 (RS): Sc in second ch from hook and in each ch across. Ch 1, turn—12 sc.

Row 2: Sc in first sc and in each sc across. Ch 1, turn.

Rows 3–19: Rep Row 2.

Fasten off, leaving a long tail for sewing.

Sprinkles

Using a long strand of Winter White and yarn needle, embroider sprinkles on the icing piece by working small backstitches randomly on the RS.

 Finishing: Center the icing piece on the toaster pastry and sew around it to attach, using the long tail left on the icing. Fasten off, weave in ends.

 You can add a little "bling" to your breakfast by sewing tiny beads to the icing for sugar sprinkles.

Lunch

Breakfast may be the most important meal of the day, but every school-aged kid knows that lunch is the best part of the day. It's a special time set aside to refuel and recharge. Lunchtime is even more fun when you have delicious food to tantalize your taste buds. Even if you don't like what's in your brown bag, odds are that you can find somebody to swap with. Your best bud might be open to trading his PB&J and Carrot for your Miniature Cheeseburger and Apple Wedges. Or the girl at the next table might just be tired enough of Sushi in her Bento box to trade you for your Pita Pocket with Falafel.

They tell us that an apple a day keeps the doctor away. I'm not entirely sure that crocheted apples are what they had in mind, but hey, it can't hurt to have a few on hand. For variety, try this in a green- or golden-colored yarn.

Apple

Ingredients

1 skein Patons Classic Wool (wool, 223 yds [203m] per 100g skein) in color Bright Red

1 skein Patons Classic Wool (wool, 223 yds [203m] per 100g skein) in color Chestnut Brown

(or comparable worsted weight yarns)

US G / 4.0mm hook

stitch marker

yarn needle

polyester fiberfill for stuffing

✳ NOTES:

- This pattern is worked in continuous rnds. Please be sure to place a marker in the first stitch of rnd.

- Apple is worked from top down.

With Bright Red, ch 2.

Rnd 1 (RS): Work 6 sc in second ch from hook—6 sc.

Rnd 2: Work 2 sc in each sc around—12 sc.

Rnd 3: [Sc in the next sc, 2 sc in next sc] six times—18 sc.

Rnd 4: [Sc in each of the next two sc, 2 sc in next sc] six times—24 sc.

Rnd 5: [Sc in each of the next three sc, 2 sc in next sc] six times—30 sc.

Rnd 6: [Sc in each of the next four sc, 2 sc in next sc] six times—36 sc.

Rnd 7: [Sc in each of the next five sc,
2 sc in next sc] six times—42 sc.

Rnds 8–11: Sc in each sc around.

Rnd 12: [Sc in each of the next five sc,
dec over next two sc] six times—36 sc.

Rnd 13: Sc in each sc around.

Rnd 14: [Sc in each of the next four sc, dec
over next two sc] six times—30 sc.

Rnds 15–17: Sc in each sc around.

Rnd 18: [Sc in each of the next three sc, dec
over next two sc] six times—24 sc.

Rnd 19: [Sc in each of the next two sc, dec over
next two sc] six times—18 sc.

Rnd 20: [Dec over two sc] nine times—9 sc.

Stuff with fiberfill.

Rnd 21: [Sc in next sc, dec over next two sc]
three times—6 sc.

Fasten off, leaving a long end for sewing. With
yarn needle, weave long end through last 6 sts,
pull tight to close. Fasten off, weave in end.

Stem

With Chestnut Brown, ch 8.

Sl st in second ch from hook and
in each ch across.

Fasten off, leaving a long tail for sewing.

❋ **Finishing:** Attach the stem to the top of the
apple using long tail and yarn nee-
dle. Pull the long end all the way
through the apple from top to bottom and pull tight to create a fairly
deep indentation in the top. Do
this a couple of times until it feels
secure. Fasten off, weave in ends.

Apples are healthy and tasty. But they aren't always easy to carry when you're low on space. I mean, can you fit a whole apple in your pocket? That's why we have apple wedges. Put one in each pocket and you're ready to snack and run.

Apple Wedge

With Winter White, ch 2.

Ingredients

1 skein Patons Classic Wool (wool, 223 yds [203m] per 100g skein) in color Bright Red

1 skein Patons Classic Wool (wool, 223 yds [203m] per 100g skein) in color Winter White

1 skein Patons Classic Wool (wool, 223 yds [203m] per 100g skein) in color Chestnut Brown

(or comparable worsted weight yarns)

US F / 3.75mm hook

yarn needle

polyester fiberfill for stuffing

Rnd 1 (RS): Work 8 sc in second ch from hook. Join with sl st to first sc—8 sc.

Rnd 2: Ch 1. Work 2 sc in same st as join and in each sc around. Join with sl st to first sc—16 sc.

Rnd 3: Ch 1. Sc in same st as join, 2 sc in next, [sc in sc, 2 sc in next sc] seven times. Join with sl st to first sc—24 sc.

Rnd 4: Ch 1. Sc in same st as join and in next sc, 2 sc in next sc, [sc in each of the next two sc, 2 sc in next sc] seven times. Join with sl st to first sc—32 sc.

Rnd 5: Ch 1. Sc in same st as join and in each of the next two sc, 2 sc in next sc, [sc in each of the next three sc, 2 sc in next sc] seven times. Join with sl st to first sc—40 sc.

Rnd 6: Ch 1. Sc in same st as join and in each of the next three sc, 2 sc in next sc, [sc in each of the next four sc, 2 sc in next sc] seven times. Join with sl st to first sc—48 sc.

Fasten off, weave in ends.

With Bright Red, ch 2.

Row 1 (WS): Sc in second ch from hook. Ch 1, turn—1 sc.

Row 2: Work 2 sc in sc. Ch 1, turn—2 sc.

Row 3: Sc in each sc across. Ch 1, turn.

Row 4: Work 2 sc in first sc, sc in next sc. Ch 1, turn—3 sc.

Row 5: Sc in each sc across. Ch 1, turn.

Row 6: Sc in first sc, 2 sc in next sc, sc in last sc. Ch 1, turn—4 sc.

Rows 7–11: Sc in each sc across. Ch 1, turn.

Row 12: Sc in each of the first two sc, 2 sc in next sc, sc in last sc. Ch 1, turn—5 sc.

Row 13: Sc in each sc across. Ch 1, turn.

Row 14: Sc in each of the first two sc, dec over next two sc, sc in last sc—4 sc.

Rows 15–19: Sc in each sc across. Ch 1, turn.

Row 20: Sc in first sc, dec over next two sc, sc in last sc. Ch 1, turn—3 sc.

Row 21: Sc in each sc across. Ch 1, turn.

Row 22: Sc in first sc, dec over next two sc. Ch 1, turn—2 sc.

Row 23: Sc in each sc across. Ch 1, turn.

Row 24: Dec over the two sc—1 sc.

Sc again in the same stitch, then continue crocheting around the side of the piece, working 2 sc in the opposite end and continuing up the other side. Join with a sl st to the first sc of the row.

Fasten off, leaving a long tail for sewing.

✳ Finishing: Join the tip of the red peel to the seam of the white circle. Match up the sts and whipstitch the two pieces tog. At the other tip of the peel, fold the white in half to form a semicircle and continue whipstitching up the other side. Stuff the piece as seam is worked. Fasten off, weave in ends.

Using a long piece of Chestnut Brown yarn, backstitch several times over one stitch near the middle of the white of the apple to create a seed. Rep several times on each side. Fasten off, weave in ends.

Did you know that if you eat massive amounts of carrots, you can end up with carotenoderma (say that three times fast!), which is a condition that causes your skin to look kind of orange? I've never eaten a crocheted carrot, but I'm pretty sure they won't change the hue of your skin!

Carrot

Ingredients

1 skein Brown Sheep Lamb's Pride Worsted (wool/mohair blend, 190 yds [173m] per 100g skein) in color Orange You Glad

1 skein Cascade 220 (wool, 220 yds [200m] per 100g skein) in color Palm

(or comparable worsted weight yarns)

US G / 4.0mm hook

stitch marker

yarn needle

polyester fiberfill for stuffing

✳ NOTES:

- This pattern is worked in continuous rnds. Please be sure to place a marker in the first stitch of rnd.

- Stuff with fiberfill as work progresses.

Carrot

With Orange You Glad, ch 2.

Rnd 1 (RS): Work 5 sc in second ch from hook—5 sc.

Rnd 2: Sc in each of the next two sc, 2 sc in next sc, sc in each of next two sc—6 sc.

Rnd 3: Sc in each sc around.

Rnd 4: [Sc in next two sc, 2 sc in next sc] two times—8 sc.

Rnd 5: Sc in each sc around.

Rnds 6–9: Rep Rnd 5.

Rnd 10: Sc in each of the next six sc, dec over next two sc—7 sc.

Rnd 11: Sc in each of the next six sc, 2 sc in next sc—8 sc.

Rnd 12: [Sc in each of the next three sc, 2 sc in next sc] two times—10 sc.

Rnd 13: Sc in each sc around.

Rnds 14–15: Rep Rnd 13.

Rnd 16: Sc in each of the first nine sc, 2 sc in next sc—11 sc.

Rnd 17: Sc in each sc around.

Rnd 18: Sc in each of the first nine sc, dec over next two sc—10 sc.

Rnd 19: [Sc in each of the first four sc, 2 sc in next] two times—12 sc.

Rnd 20: Sc in each sc around.

Rnds 21–22: Rep Rnd 20.

Rnd 23: [Sc in each of the first five sc, 2 sc in next sc] two times—14 sc.

Rnd 24: Sc in each sc around.

Rnds 25–27: Rep Rnd 24.

Rnd 28: Sc in each of the first twelve sc, dec over next two sc—13 sc.

Rnd 29: Sc in each of the first twelve sc, 2 sc in next sc—14 sc.

Rnd 30: [Sc in each of the first six sc, 2 sc in next sc] two times—16 sc.

Rnd 31: Sc in each sc around.

Rnds 32–33: Rep Rnd 31.

Rnd 34: [Dec over next two sc] eight times—8 sc.

Rnd 35: [Dec over next two sc] four times—4 sc.
Fasten off, leaving a long end for sewing.

With yarn needle, weave long end through last 4 sts, pull tight to close. Fasten off, weave in ends.

Greens

With Palm, ch 24. Fasten off.

Count back 11 ch from the end of ch 24. Join yarn in that eleventh ch. Ch 10. Fasten off. Join yarn in the next ch to the left of the eleventh ch, this time leaving a very long tail for sewing. Ch 10. Fasten off.

Finishing: With yarn needle, sew the long tail through the four long ends of the greens at the base to secure tog. Attach that to the top of the carrot. Wrap the long tail around the base of the greens to create a nice clean look. Fasten off, weave in ends.

Trim the tops of the greens down after pulling tight to be sure the chains won't unravel.

This wee cheeseburger is a delightful addition to your crochet food collection. You can even throw on some bacon (page 11), lettuce (page 59) and a tomato slice (page 59) to create a sandwich that would make any burger connoisseur proud.

Miniature Cheeseburger

Ingredients

1 skein Patons Classic Wool (wool, 223 yds [203m] per 100g skein) in color Camel

1 skein Patons Classic Wool (wool, 223 yds [203m] per 100g skein) in color Winter White

1 skein Patons Classic Wool (wool, 223 yds [203m] per 100g skein) in color Chestnut Brown

1 skein Lion Brand Lion Wool (wool, 158 yds [144m] per 85g skein) in color Goldenrod

(or comparable worsted weight yarns)

US G / 4.0mm crochet hook

yarn needle

polyester fiberfill for stuffing

 NOTE:

- Top bun is worked in two separate pieces then stitched together.

Top Bun

With Camel, ch 2.

Rnd 1 (RS): Work 12 sc in second ch from hook. Join with sl st to first sc, ch 1—12 sc.

Rnd 2: Sc in same st as join and in next sc, 3 sc in next sc, [sc in each of the next 2 sc, 3 sc in next sc] three times. Join with sl st to first sc, ch 1—20 sc.

Rnd 3: Sc in same st as join and in each of the next two sc, 3 sc in next sc, [sc in each of the next 4 sc, 3 sc in next sc] three times, sc in next sc. Join with sl st to first sc, ch 1—28 sc.

Rnd 4: Sc in same st as join and in each of the next 27 sc. Join with sl st to first sc, ch 1.

Rnd 5: Sc in same st as join and in each of the next three sc, 3 sc in next sc, [sc in each of the next 6 sc, 3 sc in next sc] three times, sc in each of the next two sc. Join with sl st to first sc, ch 1 —36 sc.

Rnd 6: Sc in same st as join and in each of the next 35 sc. Join with sl st to first sc, ch 1—35 sc.

Rnds 7–8: Rep Rnd 6.

Fasten off, weave in ends.

With Winter White, ch 2.

Rnd 1 (RS): Work 12 sc in second ch from hook. Join with sl st to first sc, ch 1—12 sc.

Rnd 2: Sc in same st as join and in next sc, 3 sc in next sc, [sc in each of the next two sc, 3 sc in next sc] three times. Join with sl st to first sc, ch 1—20 sc.

Rnd 3: Sc in same st as join and in each of the next two sc, 3 sc in next sc, [sc in each of the next four sc, 3 sc in next sc] three times, sc in next sc. Join with sl st to first sc, ch 1—28 sc.

Rnd 4: Sc in same st as join and in each of the next twenty-seven sc. Join with sl st to first sc, ch 1.

Rnd 5: Sc in same st as join and in each of the next three sc, 3 sc in next sc, [sc in each of the next six sc, 3 sc in next sc] three times, sc in each of the next two sc. Join with sl st to first sc, ch 1—36 sc.

Fasten off, leaving a long tail for sewing.

✳ Finishing: With RS facing out, match up the sts in the Camel portion and White portion and stitch tog. Lightly stuff the piece before it is fully closed. Fasten off, weave in ends.

Bottom Bun

Work Camel portion as for Top Bun up through Rnd 5.

Rnd 6: Working in the back loops only, sc in same st as join and in each of the next 35 sc. Join with sl st to first sc, ch 1—36 sc.

Rnd 7: Rep Rnd 6.

Work Winter White portion as for Top Bun.

Attach the two pieces tog as for Top Bun, but do not stuff with polyester fiberfill.

Meat Patty

Make two:

With Chestnut Brown, ch 2.

Rnd 1 (RS): Work 10 sc in second ch from hook. Join with sl st to first sc, ch 1—10 sc.

Rnd 2: Work 2 sc in same st as join and in next 9 sc. Join with sl st to first sc, ch 1—20 sc.

Rnd 3: Sc in same st as join, 2 sc in next sc, [sc in next sc, 2 sc in next sc] nine times. Join with sl st to first sc, ch 1—30 sc.

Rnd 4: Sc in same st as join and in next sc, 2 sc in next sc, [sc in each of the next two sc, 2 sc in next sc] nine times. Join with sl st to first sc, ch 1—40 sc.

Rnd 5: Sc in same st as join and in next 39 sc. Join with sl st to first sc. Fasten off, leaving a long tail for sewing.

Put the two pieces tog with RS facing out. Using the long tail and yarn needle, whipstitch around the pieces to secure. Fasten off, weave in ends.

Cheese

With Goldenrod, rep as for Top Bun, Rnds 1–5. Fasten off, weave in ends.

 **Finishing:** Assemble into cheeseburger.

Don't have a sushi bar near you? Don't fret, you can make some delicious Nigiri Sushi right in your own home, and you don't have to worry about cross contamination. It may not taste as good, but it sure does look pretty.

Nigiri Sushi

Ingredients

1 skein Patons Classic Wool (wool, 223 yds [203m] per 100g skein) in color Rich Red

1 skein Patons Classic Wool (wool, 223 yds [203m] per 100g skein) in color Winter White

1 skein Patons Classic Wool (wool, 223 yds [203m] per 100g skein) in color Deep Olive

1 skein Lion Brand Lion Wool (wool, 158 yds [144m] per 85g skein) in color Goldenrod

(or comparable worsted weight yarns)

US F / 3.75mm hook

yarn needle

polyester fiberfill for stuffing

Tamago (Egg) Nigiri

Rice

With Winter White, ch 6.

Row 1 (RS): Sc in second ch from hook and in each ch across. Ch 1, turn—5 sc.

Rnd 2: Work 2 sc in first sc, sc in each of the next three sc, work 2 sc in last sc. Continue on around to the other side of the piece, working in the free loops of the foundation ch as follows: 2 sc in first, sc in each of next three sc, 2 sc in last sc. Join with sl st to first sc—14 sc.

Rnd 3: Ch 1, sc in the same st as join and in each sc around. Join with sl st to first sc.

Rnd 4: Ch 1, sc in same st as join and in next sc, 2 sc in next sc, sc in next sc, 2 sc in next sc, sc in each of the next nine sc. Join with sl st to first sc—16 sc.

Rnd 5: Ch 1, sc in same st as join and in each st around. Join with sl st to first sc. (16 sc)

Rnd 6: Rep Rnd 5.

Rnd 7: Ch 1, Sc in same st as join and in next three sc, 2 sc in next sc, sc in next sc, 2 sc in next sc, sc in each of the next nine sc. Join with sl st to first sc—18 sc.

Rnd 8: Ch 1, sc in same st as join and in each st around. Join with sl st to first sc.

Rnd 9: Rep Rnd 8.

Rnd 10: Ch 1, sc in same st as join and in next three sc, dec over next two sc, sc in next sc, dec over next two sc, sc in each of the next nine sc. Join with sl st to first sc—16 sc.

Rnd 11: Ch 1, sc in same st as join and in each st around. Join with sl st to first sc.

Rnd 12: Rep Rnd 11.

Rnd 13: Ch 1, sc in same st as join and in next two sc, dec over next two sc, sc in next sc, dec over next two sc, sc in each of the next eight sc. Join with sl st to first sc—14 sc.

Rnd 14: Ch 1, sc in same st as join and in each st around. Join with sl st to first sc.

Rnd 15: Rep Rnd 14.

Stuff with polyester fiberfill.

Row 16: Ch 1, turn, sc in join and in next five sc. Fasten off, leaving a long tail for sewing. Fold up the flap that Row 16 made and sew the piece closed. Fasten off, weave in ends.

Egg

With Goldenrod, ch 15.

Row 1 (RS): Sc in second ch from hook and each ch across. Ch 1, turn—14 sc.

Row 2: Sc in first st and in each sc across. Ch 1, turn.

Rows 3–6: Rep Row 2.

Fasten off, leaving a long tail for sewing.

Stack the two pieces on top of each other, lining up the stitching and sew tog to make one double-thick piece of egg. Fasten off, weave in ends.

Nori Strip

With Deep Olive, ch 16.

Row 1 (RS): Sc in second ch from hook and in each ch across—15 sc. Fasten off, leaving a long tail for sewing

Finishing: Place the tamago (egg) on top of the rice. Wrap the nori strip around the nigiri (rice and egg stack). Using yarn needle, secure the two ends of the nori strip tog to secure. Fasten off, weave in ends.

Maguro (Tuna) Nigiri

Rice

Make as for Tamago Nigiri.

Tuna

With Rich Red, ch 2.

Row 1 (RS): Sc in second ch from hook. Ch 1, turn—1 sc.

Row 2: Work 2 sc in sc. Ch 1, turn—2 sc.

Row 3: Sc in first sc and in next sc.

Row 4: Work 2 sc in first sc and in next sc. Ch 1, turn—4 sc.

Row 5: Sc in first sc and in each sc across. Ch 1, turn.

Row 6: Work 2 sc in first sc, sc in each of the next two sc, 2 sc in last sc. Ch 1, turn—6 sc.

Row 7: Sc in first sc and in each sc across. Ch 1, turn.

Rows 8–12: Rep Row 7.

Row 13: Sc in first sc and in next four sc, work 3 sc in last sc—8 sc.

Continue crocheting around the piece, working 1 sc in the end of each row and 3 sc in each corner. Join with a sl st to the second sc of the first 3 sc set. Fasten off, leaving a long tail for sewing.

Finishing: Place the tuna on top of the rice and sew around to secure using the long tail of the tuna. Fasten off, weave in ends.

PB&J sandwiches are a childhood favorite that I couldn't leave out of the lunch menu. Use red yarn for the jelly if you prefer strawberry, or use white to make a "fluffernutter" (marshmallow crème and peanut butter) sandwich.

Peanut Butter & Jelly Sandwich

Ingredients

1 skein Lion Brand Fisherman's Wool (wool, 465 yds [425m] per 227g skein) in color Natural

1 skein Patons Classic Wool (wool, 223 yds [203m] per 100g skein) in color Camel

1 skein Patons Classic Wool (wool, 223 yds [203m] per 100g skein) in color Old Gold

1 skein Cascade 220 (wool, 220 yds [200m] per 100g skein) in color Grape Jelly

(or comparable worsted weight yarns)

US G / 4.0mm hook

yarn needle

Bread

Make four:

With Winter White, ch 18.

Row 1 (RS): Sc in second ch from hook and in each ch across. Ch 1, turn—17 sc.

Row 2: Sc in first sc and in each sc across. Ch 1, turn.

Rows 3–18: Rep Row 2.

Row 19: Work 6 sc in first sc, sc in next fifteen sc, work 6 sc in last sc—27 sc.

Fasten off. With RS facing, join Camel in any sc along the top edge. Sc all the way around the piece, working two sc in each of the bottom corners. Fasten off, weave in ends.

Peanut Butter and Jelly

Make two
(one in Old Gold, and one in Grape Jelly)

Ch 18.

Row 1 (RS): Sc in second ch from hook and in each ch across. Ch 1, turn—17 sc.

Row 2: 3 sc in first sc, sc across. Ch 1, turn—19 sc.

Row 3: Dec over first two sc, sc in next sixteen sc, 2 sc in last sc. Ch 1, turn.

Row 4: Sc in first seventeen sc, dec over last two sc. Ch 1, turn—18 sc.

Row 5: Sc in each sc across. Ch 1, turn.

Row 6: Dec over first two sc, sc in remaining sc across. Ch 1, turn—17 sc.

Row 7: 3 sc in first sc, sc in next fourteen, dec over last two sc. Ch 1, turn—18 sc.

Row 8: Dec over first two sc, sc in remaining sc across. Ch 1, turn—17 sc.

Row 9: 2 sc in first sc, sc in next sixteen sc. Ch 1, turn—18 sc.

Row 10: 2 sc in first sc, sc in next fourteen sc. Do not continue on to the end. Ch 1, turn—16 sc.

Row 11: Sc in first 15 sc, 2 sc in last sc. Ch 1, turn—17 sc.

Row 12: 2 sc in first sc, sc in next sixteen sc. Ch 1, turn—18 sc.

Row 13: 2 sc in first sc, sc in next seventeen sc. Ch 1, turn—19 sc.

Row 14: 2 sc in first sc, sc in next eighteen sc. Ch 1, turn—20 sc.

Row 15: 2 sc in first sc, sc in next seventeen sc, dec over last two sc. Ch 1, turn.

Row 16: Dec over first two sc, sc in next eighteen sc. Ch 1, turn—19 sc.

Row 17: Dec over first two sc, sc in next fifteen sc, dec over last two sc. Ch 1, turn—17 sc.

Row 18: Dec over first two sc, sc in next fifteen sc, dec over last two sc. Ch 1, turn—15 sc.

Fasten off, weave in ends. Block flat.

❋ Finishing: Pin two of the pieces of bread tog with RS facing. Using Camel, sew through both pieces all the way around. Fasten off, weave in ends. Block flat.

Place peanut butter and jelly pieces between bread slices.

A peanut is a magical snack. It comes in its own biodegradable wrapper, it's portable and it's yummy. Not to mention it's the munchie of choice at baseball games.

Peanuts

Ingredients

1 skein Yarn Source Sol (wool, 220 yds [200m] per 100g skein) in color Tan

(or comparable worsted weight yarn)

US F / 3.75mm hook

yarn needle

polyester fiberfill for stuffing

With Tan, ch 2.

Rnd 1 (RS): Work 4 sc in second ch from hook. Join with sl st to first sc, ch 1—4 sc.

Rnd 2: Sc in same st as join, 2 sc in next sc, sc in next sc, 2 sc in next sc. Join with sl st to first sc, ch 1—6 sc.

Rnd 3: Sc in same st as join, 2 sc in next sc, [sc in next sc, 2 sc in next sc] two times. Join with sl st to first sc, ch 1—9 sc.

Rnd 4: Sc in same st as join and in the next eight sc. Join with sl st to first sc, ch 1.

Rnd 5: Rep Rnd 4.

Rnd 6: Sc in same st as join, dec over next two sc, [sc in next sc, dec over next two sc] two times. Join with sl st to first sc, ch 1—6 sc.

Rnd 7: Sc in same st as join and in the next five sc. Join with sl st to first sc, ch 1.

Rnd 8: Sc in same st as join, 2 sc in next sc, [sc in next sc, 2 sc in next sc] two times. Join with sl st to first sc, ch 1—9 sc.

Rnd 9: Sc in same st as join and in the next eight sc. Join with sl st to first sc, ch 1.

Row 10: Sc in same st as join and in the next eight sc. Join with sl st to first sc, ch 1.

Rnd 11: Sc in same st as join, dec over next two sc, [sc in next sc, dec over next two sc] two times. Join with sl st to first sc, ch 1—6 sc.

Rnd 12: Sc in same st as join, dec over next two sc, sc in next sc, dec over next two sc. Join with sl st to first sc—4 sc.

Stuff with polyester fiberfill.

Finishing: Fasten off, leaving a long tail for sewing. Using yarn needle, weave the long tail through the remaining 4 sts and pull tight to close. Fasten off, weave in ends.

You'll never have to chase these crocheted peas around your plate with a knife and fork! If you want a bigger pile o' peas, just make a longer starting chain and work the whole thing in the pattern.

Peas

Ingredients

1 skein Patons Classic Wool (wool, 223 yds [203m] per 100g skein) in color

Leaf Green

(or comparable worsted weight yarn)

US G / 4.0mm hook

yarn needle

Special Stitch:

YO and insert hook into desired st. Pull up a loop. YO and draw through two loops—2 loops left on hook. YO and insert hook into same st, pull up a loop. YO and pull through two loops—3 loops left on hook. YO and insert hook into same st, pull up a loop. YO and pull through two loops—4 loops left on hook. YO and insert hook into same st, pull up a loop. YO and pull through two loops—5 loops left on hook. YO and pull through all five loops on the hook—1 Pea Stitch (PS) completed.

Ch 56.

Row 1 (RS): PS in second ch from hook, sc in next ch, [PS in next ch, sc in next] across, ending with PS in last ch—28 PS and 27 sc.

Fasten off, leaving a long tail for sewing.

Finishing: Start coiling the long strand of peas around itself, sewing in place using yarn needle and the long tail of yarn. Take care to place each successive round slightly below the row before it to end up with a "pile" of peas. Fasten off, weave in ends.

There is a lovely little Greek restaurant down the street from where I live, and falafel is my absolute favorite menu item. My children prefer to eat cheeseburgers when we go out, but they love to play with their crocheted pita pocket and falafels.

Pita Pocket with Falafel

Ingredients

1 skein Patons Classic Wool (wool, 223 yds [203m] per 100g skein) in color Camel

1 skein Patons Classic Wool (wool, 223 yds [203m] per 100g skein) in color Chestnut Brown

1 skein Patons Classic Wool (wool, 223 yds [203m] per 100g skein) in color Bright Red

1 skein Patons Classic Wool (wool, 223 yds [203m] per 100g skein) in color Leaf Green

(or comparable worsted weight yarns)

US G / 4.0mm hook

stitch marker

yarn needle

polyester fiberfill for stuffing

Pita Pocket

Make two:

With Camel, ch 2.

Row 1 (RS): Work 3 sc in second ch from hook. Ch 1, turn—3 sc.

Row 2: Work 2 sc in each sc across. Ch 1, turn—6 sc.

Row 3: Sc in the first sc, 2 sc in next sc, [sc in next sc, 2 sc in next sc] twice. Ch 1, turn—9 sc.

Row 4: Sc in each of the first two sc, 2 sc in next sc, [sc in each of the next two sc, 2 sc in next sc] twice. Ch 1, turn—12 sc.

Row 5: Sc in each of the first three sc, 2 sc in next sc, [sc in each of the next three sc, 2 sc in next sc] twice. Ch 1, turn—15 sc.

Row 6: Sc in each of the first four sc, 2 sc in next sc, [sc in each of the next four sc, 2 sc in next sc] twice. Ch 1, turn—18 sc.

Row 7: Sc in each of the first five sc, 2 sc in next sc, [sc in each of the next five sc, 2 sc in next sc] twice. Ch 1, turn—21 sc.

Row 8: Sc in each of the first six sc, 2 sc in next sc, [sc in each of the next six sc, 2 sc in next sc] twice. Ch 1, turn—24 sc.

Row 9: Sc in each of the first seven sc, 2 sc in next sc, [sc in each of the next seven sc, 2 sc in next sc] twice. Ch 1, turn—27 sc.

Row 10: Sc in each of the first eight sc, 2 sc in next sc, [sc in each of the next eight sc, 2 sc in next sc] twice. Ch 1, turn—30 sc.

Row 11: Sc in each of the first nine sc, 2 sc in next sc, [sc in each of the next nine sc, 2 sc in next sc] twice. Ch 1, turn—33 sc.

Row 12: Sc in each of the first ten sc, 2 sc in next sc, [sc in each of the next ten sc, 2 sc in next sc] twice. Ch 1, turn—36 sc.

Row 13: Sc in each of the first eleven sc, 2 sc in next sc, [sc in each of the next eleven sc, 2 sc in next sc] twice. Ch 1, turn—39 sc.

Row 14: Sc in each of the first twelve sc, 2 sc in next sc, [sc in each of the next twelve sc, 2 sc in next sc] twice. Sc again into the last st. Do not turn. Continue around the corner and crochet along the straight edge, working 1 sc into the end of each row across. Ch 1, turn—71 sc.

Row 15: Sc in each sc across to the corner. Ch 1, turn—28 sc.

Row 16: Sc in each sc across, working 2 sc in last st. Do not turn. Continue on around the corner, working 1 sc into each row end and each sc around. Join with sl st to the first st of Row 16—71 sc.

Fasten off, weave in ends.

 Finishing: Taking care to match up the sts along the edge, pin the two pieces tog with RS facing. Using G hook, join Camel in one corner, and crochet the two pieces tog by working 1 sc in each sc around the curved edge, ending at the opposite corner. Fasten off, weave in ends. Block flat.

Falafel

 NOTE:

- This pattern is worked in continuous rnds. Please be sure to place a marker in the first stitch of rnd.

With Chestnut Brown, ch 2.

Rnd 1 (RS): Work 6 sc in second ch from hook—6 sc.

Rnd 2: Work 2 sc in each sc around—12 sc.

Rnd 3: [Sc in next sc, 2 sc in next sc] six times—18 sc.

Rnd 4: [Sc in each of the next two sc, 2 sc in next sc] six times—24 sc.

Rnd 5: [Sc in each of the next three sc, 2 sc in next sc] six times—30 sc.

Rnd 6: Sc in each sc around.

Rnds 7–8: Rep Rnd 6.

Rnd 9: [Sc in each of the next three sc, dec over next two sc] six times—24 sc.

Rnd 10: [Sc in each of the next two sc, dec over next two sc] six times—18 sc.

Rnd 11: [Sc in next sc, dec over next two sc] six times—12 sc.

Stuff with polyester fiberfill.

Rnd 12: [Dec over next two sc] six times—6 sc. Fasten off, leaving a long end for sewing.

Using yarn needle, weave yarn through the last 6 sc. Pull tight. Fasten off, weave in ends.

Tomato Slice

Make two:

With Bright Red, ch 2.

Rnd 1: Work 10 sc in second ch from hook. Join with sl st to first sc—10 sc.

Rnd 2: Ch 1. Work 2 sc in the same st as join and in next nine sc. Join with sl st to first sc—20 sc.

Rnd 3: Ch 1. Sc in same st as join, 2 sc in next sc, [sc in next sc, 2 sc in next sc] nine times. Join with sl st to first sc—30 sc.

Rnd 4: Ch 1. Sc in same st as join and in next twenty-nine sc. Join with sl st to first sc.

Fasten, leaving a long end for sewing.

Fold the tomato slice in half, matching up the sts and sew around to secure. Fasten off, weave in ends.

Lettuce

Make two:

With Leaf Green, ch 2.

Rnd 1 (RS): Work 10 sc in second ch from hook. Join with sl st to first sc—10 sc.

Rnd 2: Ch 1. Work 2 sc in the same st as join and in next nine sc. Join with sl st to first sc—20 sc.

Rnd 3: Ch 1. Sc in same st as join, 2 sc in next sc, sc in next sc, 2 sc in next sc, work 2 dc in each of the next twelve sc, [2 sc in next sc, sc in next sc] two times. Join with sl st to first sc—36 sts.

Rnd 4: Ch 1. Sc in same st as join and in each of the next nine sts, [2 dc in next st, 3 dc in next st] eight times, sc in each of the next ten sts. Join with sl st to first sc—60 sts.

Rnd 5: Ch 1. Sc in same st as join and in each of the next 13 sts, dc in each of the next thirty-two sts, sc in each of the next fourteen sts. Join with sl st to first sc.

Fasten off, weave in ends.

❋ **Finishing:** Place the falafel, tomato and lettuce into the pita pocket.

You've got all four food groups here in one sandwich! Pack this in a brown bag with some Apple Wedges (page 33) and Chocolate Chip Cookies (page 109) for a lunch any fourth grader would love to have.

Salami & Swiss on Whole Wheat

Ingredients

1 skein Patons Classic Wool (wool, 223 yds [203m] per 100g skein) in color Camel

1 skein Patons Classic Wool (wool, 223 yds [203m] per 100g skein) in color Chestnut Brown

1 skein Lion Brand Fisherman's Wool (wool, 465 yds [425m] per 227g skein) in color Natural

1 skein Lion Brand Wool-Ease (wool/acrylic/polyester blend, 197 yds [179m] per 85g skein) in color Chestnut Heather

1 skein Patons Classic Wool (wool, 223 yds [203m] per 100g skein) in color Bright Red

1 skein Patons Classic Wool (wool, 223 yds [203m] per 100g skein) in color Leaf Green

(or comparable worsted weight yarn)

US G / 4mm hook

US F / 3.75mm hook

yarn needle

polyester fiberfill for stuffing

Swiss Cheese

With Natural and G hook, ch 21.

Row 1 (RS): Sc in second ch from hook and in each ch across. Ch 1, turn—20 sc.

Row 2: Sc in first sc and in each sc across. Ch 1, turn.

Row 3: Sc in each of the first three sc, ch 4, skip next four sc, sc across to end. Ch 1, turn —16 sc, 4 ch.

Row 4: Sc in each of the first thirteen sc, ch 4, sc in last three sc. Ch 1, turn.

Row 5: Sc in each of the first three sc, ch 4, sc in last thirteen sc. Ch 1, turn.

Row 6: Sc in each of the first thirteen sc, 4 sc in the ch-4 sp of Row 3, sc in last three sc. Ch 1, turn—20 sc.

Row 7: Sc in each sc across. Ch 1, turn.

Row 8: Rep Row 7.

Row 9: Sc in each of the first fourteen sc, ch 4, skip next four sc, sc in last two sc. Ch 1, turn—16 sc, 4 ch.

Row 10: Sc in each of the first two sc, ch 4, sc in last fourteen sc. Ch 1, turn.

Row 11: Sc in each of the first fourteen sc, 4 sc in the ch-4 sp of Row 9, sc in last two sc. Ch 1, turn—20 sc.

Row 12: Sc in each sc across. Ch 1, turn.

Row 13: Rep Row 12.

Row 14: Sc in each of the first eighteen sc, do not work in the last two sc. Ch 1, turn—18 sc.

Row 15: Sc in each sc across. Ch 1, turn.

Row 16: Sc in each of the first seventeen sc, 2 sc in last sc. Ch 1, turn—19 sc.

Row 17: Work 2 sc in first sc, sc in each sc to end. Ch 1, turn—20 sc.

Row 18: Sc in each sc across. Ch 1, turn.

Row 19: Rep Row 18.

Row 20: Sc in each of the first seven sc, ch 5, skip next five sc, sc in last eight sc. Ch 1, turn—15 sc, 5 ch.

Row 21: Sc in each of the first eight sc, ch 5, sc in last seven sc. Ch 1, turn.

Row 22: Sc in each of the first seven sc, ch 5, sc in last eight sc. Ch 1, turn.

Row 23: Sc in each of the first eight sc, 5 sc in the ch-5 sp of Row 20, sc in last seven sc—20 sc.

Fasten off, weave in ends.

Salami

Make two:

With Chestnut Heather and G hook, ch 2.

Rnd 1: Work 10 sc in second ch from hook. Join with sl st to first sc, ch 1—10 sc.

Rnd 2: Work 2 sc in same st as join and in next nine sc. Join with sl st to first sc, ch 1—20 sc.

Rnd 3: Sc in same st as join and in each sc across. Join with sl st to first sc, ch 1.

Rnd 4: Sc in same st as join, 2 sc in next sc, [sc in next sc, 2 sc in next sc] nine times. Join with sl st to first sc, ch 1—30 sc.

Rnd 5: Sc in same st as join and in next sc, 2 sc in next sc, [sc in each of the next two sc, 2 sc in next sc] nine times. Join with sl st to first sc, ch 1—40 sc.

Rnd 6: Sc in same st as join and in each of the next two sc, work 2 sc in next sc, [sc in each of the next three sc, 2 sc in next sc] nine times. Join with sl st to first sc, ch 1—50 sc.

Rnd 7: Sc in same st as join and in each sc of the next forty-nine sc. Join with sl st to first sc.

Fasten off, weave in ends.

Lettuce

With Leaf Green and G hook, work as for Falafel Pita Pocket (page 57).

Tomato Slice

Make two:

With Bright Red and F hook, ch 4. Join with sl st to form a ring.

Rnd 1: Ch 2. Hdc into ring, [2 hdc, ch 1] seven times. Sl st into first hdc to join—15 hdc.

Rnd 2: Sl st into next ch-1 sp, ch 3, dc into same sp as sl st, ch 2, [2 dc, ch 2 into next ch-1 sp] seven times. Join with sl st into third ch of ch 3.

Rnd 3: Ch 1, sc in same st as join and in each dc and ch around.

Fasten off, weave in ends.

Bread

Make as for Peanut Butter & Jelly Sandwich (page 49), using Camel for main body of bread and Chestnut Brown for crust and G hook.

 Finishing: Place cheese, salami, lettuce and tomato between bread slices.

Maki-zushi, or sushi rolls, are what comes to mind when most people think of sushi. Make them together with the Nigiri Sushi from page 45 for a Japanese feast.

Sushi Rolls

Ingredients

1 skein Patons Classic Wool (wool, 223 yds [203m] per 100g skein) in color Deep Olive

1 skein Patons Classic Wool (wool, 223 yds [203m] per 100g skein) in color Winter White

1 skein Patons Classic Wool (wool, 223 yds [203m] per 100g skein) in color Rich Red

1 skein Patons Classic Wool (wool, 223 yds [203m] per 100g skein) in color Leaf Green

1 skein Yarn Source Sol (wool, 220 yds [200m] per 100g skein) in color Orange

(or comparable worsted weight yarn)

US F / 3.75mm hook

yarn needle

polyester fiberfill for stuffing

Tuna Roll

Make two:

With Rich Red, ch 2

Rnd 1 (RS): Work 5 sc in second ch from hook. Join with sl st to first sc. Change to Winter White. Ch 1—5 sc.

Rnd 2: Work 2 sc in same st as join, work 2 sc in each of the next four sc. Join with sl st to first sc, ch 1—10 sc.

Rnd 3: Sc in same st as join, 2 sc in next sc, [sc in next sc, 2 sc in next sc] four times. Join with sl st to first sc, ch 1—15 sc.

Fasten off, weave in ends.

With Deep Olive, ch 17.

Row 1 (RS): Sc in second ch from hook and in each ch across. Ch 1, turn—16 sc.

Row 2: Sc in first sc and each sc across.

Rows 3–6: Rep Row 2.

Fasten off, leaving a very long tail for sewing.

 Finishing: Using the yarn needle and the long tail, attach the green portion to one of the rounds by sewing across the long end, taking care that the RS of the round portion is facing. Continue sewing down the short side of the green portion, attaching the two ends tog. Then, attach the other round portion, again taking care that the RS is facing. Stuff the piece before it is fully closed.Fasten off, weave in ends.

Carrot Roll

Make as for Tuna Roll, using Orange for Row 1.

Avocado Roll

Make as for Tuna Roll, using Leaf Green for Row 1.

 Get creative with yarn color to make many different types of sushi, and don't forget to invite me over when you've got the entire buffet ready!

Tomatoes are a summer staple at our house. There are so many ways to use them, and we include them in most of our meals when they're in season. Sometimes our tomato plants don't do so well, though, and I have to whip up a few to keep the basil company.

Tomato

Ingredients

1 skein Patons Classic Wool (wool, 223 yds [203m] per 100g skein) in color Bright Red

1 skein Cascade 220 (wool, 220 yds [200m] per 100g skein) in color Palm

(or comparable worsted weight yarns)

US G / 4.0mm hook

stitch marker

yarn needle

polyester fiberfill for stuffing

❋ NOTES:

• This pattern is worked in continuous rounds. Please be sure to place your stitch marker in the first stitch of round.

• Tomato is worked from top down.

With Bright Red, ch 2.

Rnd 1 (RS): Work 8 sc in second ch from hook—8 sc.

Rnd 2: Work 2 sc in each sc around—16 sc.

Rnd 3: [Sc in the next sc, 2 sc in next sc] eight times—24 sc.

Rnd 4: [Sc in each of the next two sc, 2 sc in next sc] eight times—32 sc.

Rnd 5: [Sc in each of the next three sc, 2 sc in next sc] eight times—40 sc.

Rnd 6: [Sc in each of the next four sc, 2 sc in next sc] eight times—48 sc.

Rnds 7–11: Sc in each sc around.

Rnd 12: [Sc in each of the next four sc, dec over next two sc] eight times—40 sc.

Rnd 13: [Sc in each of the next three sc, dec over next two sc] eight times—32 sc.

Rnd 14: [Sc in each of the next two sc, dec over next two sc] eight times—24 sc.

Rnd 15: Sc in each sc around.

Rnd 16: [Sc in next sc, dec over next two sc] eight times—16 sc.

Rnd 17: [Sc in each of the next two sc, dec over next two sc] four times—12 sc.

Stuff with fiberfill.

Rnd 18: [Dec over next two sc] six times—6 sc.

Fasten off, leaving a long end for sewing. With yarn needle, weave long end through last six stitches and pull tight to close. Tie off and weave in end.

With Palm, ch 2.

Rnd 1: Work five sc in second ch from hook. Join with sl st to first sc.

Rnd 2: *Ch 3, sl st in second ch from hook and next ch, sl st in same st as ch 3; rep from * four times. Fasten off, leaving a long tail for sewing.

✳ **Finishing:** Attach the green stem to the top of the tomato using long tail and yarn needle. Pull the long end all the way through the tomato from top to bottom and pull tight to create a slight indentation in the top. You can do this a couple of times until it feels secure. Tie off yarn. Weave in ends.

Cherry Tomatoes on the Vine

Ingredients

1 skein Patons Classic Wool (wool, 223 yds [203m] per 100g skein) in color Bright Red

1 skein Cascade 220 (wool, 220 yds [200m] per 100g skein) in color Palm

(or comparable worsted weight yarns)

US G / 4.0mm Hook

US E / 3.5mm Hook

stitch marker

yarn needle

polyester fiberfill for stuffing

✳ **NOTES:**

- This pattern is worked in continuous rnds. Please be sure to place a marker in the first stitch of rnd.

- Tomato is worked from top down.

Tomato

Make three:

With Bright Red and G hook, ch 2.

Rnd 1 (RS): Work 6 sc in second ch from hook—6 sc.

Rnd 2: Work 2 sc in each sc around—12 sc.

Row 3: [Sc in the next sc, 2 sc in next sc] six times—18 sc.

Rnds 4–6: Sc in each sc around.

Rnds 7: [Sc, dec over next two sc] six times—12 sc.

Rnd 8: [Dec over the next two sc] six times—6 sc.

Stuff with fiberfill.

Fasten off, leaving a long end for sewing. With yarn needle, weave long end through last 6 sts pull tight to close. Fasten off, weave in ends.

Greens

With Palm and E hook, ch 2.

Rnd 1: Work four sc in second ch from hook. Join with sl st to first sc.

Rnd 2: *Ch 4, sl st in second ch from hook and next two ch, sl st in same st as ch 3; rep from * in remaining three sc. Fasten off, leaving a long tail for sewing.

Attach the green stem to the top of the tomato using long tail and yarn needle. Fasten off, weave in ends.

Vines

With Palm and E hook, ch 10 very tightly, leaving long tails at both ends. Attach one of the ends to the center of the greens in the top of one of the cherry tomatoes. Rep for each tomato.

Ch 25 tightly. This is the main vine. Attach three tomatoes to this at even intervals. Fasten off, weave in ends.

Dinner

One of the most asked questions (right behind "What is the meaning of life?") is "What's for dinner?" Well, that depends. Are you looking for a casual get together with friends? If so, then Pizza and a Side Salad are what you need. If you want something a little fancier, try the Chicken Drumstick, some Green Beans, and Mushrooms. Eating dinner on the fly tonight? Grab a Taco, and you'll be good to go. If your taste buds are crying out for something a little more sophisticated, try wrapping some Bacon (page 11) around your Asparagus. Or crochet it all and serve it up buffet style.

I love seeing asparagus in the produce department, because the arrival of those tender young shoots means that spring is here. Traditional green asparagus is featured here, but if your tastes are more adventurous, whip up some stalks in white or purple hues.

Asparagus

Ingredients

1 skein Patons Classic Wool (wool, 223 yds [203m] per 100g skein) in color Deep Olive

1 skein Yarn Source Sol (wool, 220 yds [200m] per 100g skein) in color Chartreuse

(or comparable worsted weight yarns)

US G / 4mm hook

US F / 3.75mm hook

stitch marker

yarn needle

polyester fiberfill for stuffing

❋ NOTES:

- A portion of this pattern is worked in continuous rnds. Please be sure to place a marker in the first stitch of rnd.
- Stuff with fiberfill as work progresses.

With one strand of Chartreuse and one strand of Deep Olive held tog and G hook, ch 2.

Rnd 1 (RS): Work 3 sc in second ch from hook. Join with sl st to first sc, ch 1—3 sc.

Rnd 2: Sc in same st as join, 2 sc in next sc, sc in next sc. Join with sl st to first sc, ch 1—4 sc.

Rnd 3: Sc in same st as join and in next sc, 2 sc in next sc, sc in next sc. Join with sl st to first sc, ch 1—5 sc.

Rnd 4: Sc in same st as join and in each of the next three sc, 2 sc in next sc. Join with sl st to first sc, ch 1—6 sc.

Break off Deep Olive and change to F hook. From this point on, the asparagus is worked in continuous rnds.

Rnd 5: Sc in same st as join and in each of the next five sc—6 sc.

Rnd 6: Sc in each sc around.

Rnds 7–11: Repeat Rnd 6.

Rnd 12: Sc in each of the first three sc, 2 sc in next sc, sc in each of the next two sc—7 sc.

Rnd 13: Sc in each sc around.

Rnd 14: Sc in each of the first two sc, 2 sc in next sc, sc in each of the next two sc, 2 sc in next sc, sc in next sc—9 sc.

Rnd 15: Sc in each sc around.

Rnds 16–27: Repeat Row 15.

Rnd 28: Sc in each of the first three sc, 2 sc in next sc, sc in each of the next three sc, 2 sc in next sc, sc in next sc—11 sc.

Rnd 29: Sc in each sc around.

Rnd 30: Working in back loop only, sc in first sc, [dec over next two sc] five times—6 sc.

Rnd 31: Working through both loops, [dec over next two sc] three times—3 sc.

Fasten off, leaving long tail for sewing.

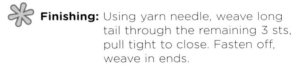 **Finishing:** Using yarn needle, weave long tail through the remaining 3 sts, pull tight to close. Fasten off, weave in ends.

 Use two different shades of purple yarn for the tip of the purple asparagus. Two shades of white for the white variety can be used too, though the result is more subtle.

I grew up in a house with four sisters, and we always argued over who got the drumstick at dinnertime. Being the middle child as well as the shortest, I never won. But now, I can have as many as I want, and I don't have to share. Nyah.

Chicken Drumstick

Ingredients

1 skein Yarn Source Sol (wool, 220 yds [200m] per 100g skein) in color Tan

1 skein Patons Classic Wool (wool, 223 yds [203m] per 100g skein) in color Winter White

(or comparable worsted weight yarns)

US F / 3.75mm hook

stitch marker

yarn needle

polyester fiberfill for stuffing

✳ NOTES:

- This pattern is worked in continuous rnds. Please be sure to place a marker in the first stitch of rnd.
- Stuff with fiberfill as work progresses.

With Tan, ch 2.

Rnd 1 (RS): Work 8 sc in second ch from hook—8 sc.

Rnd 2: Work 2 sc in each sc around—16 sc.

Rnd 3: [Sc in the next sc, 2 sc in next sc] six times—24 sc.

Rnd 4: [Sc in each of the next three sc, 2 sc in next sc] six times—30 sc.

Rnds 5-9: Sc in each sc around.

Rnd 10: [Sc in each of the next eight sc, dec over next two sc] three times—27 sc.

Rnd 11: Sc in each sc around.

Rnd 12: [Sc in each of the next seven sc, dec over next two sc] three times—24 sc.

Rnd 13: Sc in each sc around.

Rnd 14: [Sc in each of the next six sc, dec over next two sc] three times—21 sc.

Rnd 15: [Sc in each of the next five sc, dec over next two sc] three times—18 sc.

Rnds 16–18: Sc in each sc around.

Rnd 19: [Sc in each of the next four sc, dec over next two sc] three times—15 sc.

Rnd 20: [Sc in each of the next three sc, dec over next two sc] three times—12 sc.

Rnds 21–23: Sc in each sc around. Cut yarn, join Winter White in next st.

Rnd 24: With Winter White, working in back loop only, sc in same st as join, dec over next two sc, [sc in next sc, dec over next two sc] three times—8 sc.

Rnd 25: Working through both loops now, sc in each sc around.

Rnds 26–27: Sc in each sc around.

Rnd 28: [Sc in each of the next three sc, 2 sc in next sc] two times—10 sc.

Rnd 29: [Sc in next sc, 2 sc in next sc] five times—15 sc.

Rnds 30–31: Sc in each sc around.

The next rows make the separation at the bone end of the drumstick.

Rnd 32: Sc in each of the next eight sc, skip next seven sc. Join with sl st to the first sc of the rnd—8 sc.

Rnd 33: Ch 1. Sc in same sc as join and in the next seven sc around. Join with sl st to the first sc of the rnd, ch 1—8 sc.

Row 34: Dec over same sc as join and next sc, [dec over next two sc] three times—4 sc.

Fasten off, leaving a long tail.

 Finishing: Using a yarn needle, weave through the remaining 4 sts, pull tight to close. Sc around the remaining free sts on the other side of the separation of the drumstick end. Rep Rnds 33 and 34. Fasten off, weave in ends.

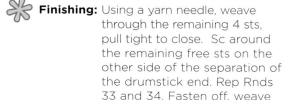
Make a complete chicken dinner that includes salad, green beans, and for desert, pumpkin pie!

I love green beans. Give them to me fresh from the garden, frozen or canned; steamed, in casseroles or roasted. I'll take them any way I can get them. Even crocheted.

Green Beans

Ingredients

1 skein Yarn Source Sol (wool, 220 yds [200m] per 100g skein) in color Chartreuse

(or comparable worsted weight yarn)

US G / 4.0mm hook

yarn needle

✳ NOTES:

- You can vary the length of the beans by making more or less chains in your foundation chain.
- These green beans can be left loose, or can be joined together. I suggest joining two beans together at a time, and then joining those groups together.

Ch 17.

Row 1 (RS): Sc in second ch from hook, and in each ch across. Ch 1, turn—16 sc.

Row 2: Sc in first sc and in each sc across. Ch 1, turn.

Rows 3–4: Rep Row 2.

Fasten off, leaving a long tail for sewing.

✳ **Finishing:** Fold the piece with the long ends tog. Sew through to join. Fasten off, weave in ends.

Delicious, nutritious and homes to fairies throughout the world, mushrooms are the only fungus welcome in most people's homes. For a bit of fun, make the cap of the mushroom red and make the stem white, and crochet it as long as you'd like.

Mushroom

Ingredients

1 skein Patons Classic Wool (wool, 223 yds [203m] per 100g skein) in color Natural Mix

1 skein Patons Classic Wool (wool, 223 yds [203m] per 100g skein) in color Black

(or comparable worsted weight yarns)

US G / 4.0mm hook

yarn needle

polyester fiberfill for stuffing

With Natural Mix, Ch 2.

Rnd 1 (RS): Work 6 sc in second ch from hook. Join with sl st to first sc—6 sc.

Rnd 2: Ch 1. Work 2 sc in same st as join and in each of the next five sc. Join with sl st to first sc—12 sc.

Rnd 3: Ch 1. Sc in same sc as join, 2 sc in next sc, [sc in next sc, 2 sc in next sc] five times. Join with sl st to first sc—18 sc.

Rnd 4: Ch 1. Sc in same sc as join, sc in next sc, 2 sc in next sc, [sc in each of the next two sc, 2 sc in next sc] five times. Join with sl st to first sc—24 sc.

Rnd 5: Ch 1. Sc in same sc as join, sc in each of next two sc, 2 sc in next sc, [sc in each of the next three sc, 2 sc in next sc] five times. Join with sl st to first sc—30 sc.

Rnd 6: Ch 1. Sc in same sc as join and in next twenty-nine sc. Join with sl st to first sc.

Rnd 7: Rep Rnd 6.

Rnd 8: Change to Black. Ch 1. Working in back loop only, dec over same st as join and next st, [dec over next two sc] fourteen times. Join with sl st to first sc—15 sc.

Rnd 9: Ch 1. Working in both loops, sc in same sc as join, dec over next two sc, [sc in next sc, dec over next two sc] four times. Join with sl st to first sc—10 sc.

Rnd 10: Change to Natural Mix. Ch 1. Sc in same st as join and in each sc around. Join with sl st to first sc—10 sc.

Stuff mushroom cap with fiberfill.

Rnd 11: Ch 1. Sc in same st as join and in each sc around. Join with sl st to first sc—10 sc.

Rnds 12–13: Rep Rnd 11.

Rnd 14: Ch 1. Working in back loop only, dec over same st as join and next sc, [dec over next two sc] four times. Join with sl st to first sc—5 sc.

Stuff with polyester fiberfill.

Fasten off, leaving a long end for sewing.

Finishing: With yarn needle, weave long end through last 5 sts, pull tight to close. Fasten off, weave in ends.

You can load your pizza up with pepperoni, make it vegetarian, or cheese only—everyone has their favorites. Lots of olives for me, please, and hold the green peppers.

Pizza

Ingredients

1 skein Patons Classic Wool (wool, 223 yds [203m] per 100g skein) in color Winter White

1 skein Patons Classic Wool (wool, 223 yds [203m] per 100g skein) in color Paprika

1 skein Patons Classic Wool (wool, 223 yds [203m] per 100g skein) in color Camel

(or comparable worsted weight yarns)

US G / 4.0mm hook

stitch markers

yarn needle

Crust

With Camel, ch 2.

Row 1 (WS): Work 2 sc in second ch from hook. Ch 1, turn—2 sc.

Row 2: Sc in each sc across. Ch 1, turn.

Row 3: Work 2 sc in first sc and in next sc. Ch 1, turn—4 sc.

Rows 4-5: Sc in each sc across. Ch 1, turn.

Row 6: Work 2 sc in first sc, sc in each of the next two sc, 2 sc in last sc. Ch 1, turn—6 sc.

Rows 7-8: Sc in each sc across. Ch 1, turn.

Row 9: Work 2 sc in first sc, sc in each of the next four sc, 2 sc in last sc. Ch 1, turn—8 sc.

Rows 10-11: Sc in each sc across. Ch 1, turn.

Row 12: Work 2 sc in first sc, sc in each of the next six sc, 2 sc in last sc. Ch 1, turn—10 sc.

Rows 13–14: Sc in each sc across. Ch 1, turn.

Row 15: Work 2 sc in first sc, sc in each of the next eight sc, 2 sc in last sc. Ch 1, turn—12 sc.

Rows 16–17: Sc in each sc across. Ch 1, turn.

Row 18: Work 2 sc in first sc, sc in each of the next ten sc, 2 sc in last sc. Ch 1, turn—14 sc.

Rows 19–20: Sc in each sc across. Ch 1, turn.

Row 21: Work 2 sc in first sc, sc in each of the next twelve sc, 2 sc in last sc. Ch 1, turn—16 sc.

Row 22–23: Sc in each sc across. Ch 1, turn.

Row 24: Work 2 sc in first sc, sc in each of the next fourteen sc, 2 sc in last sc. Ch 1, turn—18 sc.

Rows 25–26: Sc in each sc across. Ch 1, turn.

Row 27: Work 2 sc in first sc, sc in each of the next sixteen sc, 2 sc in last sc. Ch 1, turn—20 sc.

Rows 28–29: Sc in each sc across. Ch 1, turn.

Row 30: Work 2 sc in first sc, sc in each of the next eighteen sc, 2 sc in last sc. Ch 1, turn—22 sc.

Place a stitch marker at each end of this row.

Rows 31–38: Sc in each sc across.

Fasten off, leaving a long end for sewing.

To form the crust, take the long end of the final row, and fold it over to Row 30, which is marked with stitch markers. Using the long tail, sew across from one side to the other to secure the crust down. Fasten off, weave in ends.

Sauce

Using Paprika, rep as for Crust to Row 30.

Fasten off, leaving a long tail for sewing.

Position the sauce on top of the crust and sew alll of the way around to attach. Take care to not sew all of the way through the crust to keep sts from showing.

Fasten off, weave in ends.

Cheese

Using Winter White, rep as for Crust to Row 30.

Fasten off, leaving a long tail for sewing.

Position the cheese on top of the sauce and sew all of the way around to attach as before.

Fasten off, weave in ends. Block flat.

Black Olives

With Ebony and E hook, ch 9 tightly. Sl st in first ch to form a ring.

Fasten off, leaving a long tail for sewing. Attach to the cheese using the long tail and yarn needle.

Pizza Toppings

Ingredients

1 skein Lion Brand Wool-Ease (wool/acrylic/polyester blend, 197 yds [179m] per 85g skein) in color Chestnut Heather

1 skein Yarn Source Sol (wool, 220 yds [200m] per 100g skein) in color Chartreuse

1 skein Lion Brand Lion Wool (wool, 158 yds [144m] per 85g skein) in color Ebony

(or comparable worsted weight yarns)

US E / 3.5mm hook

US F / 3.75mm hook

US G / 4.0mm hook

yarn needle

Green Peppers

With Chartreuse and F hook, ch 10.

Row 1 (RS): Sl st in second ch from hook and in each ch across.

Fasten off, leaving a long tail for sewing. Attach to the cheese using the long tail and yarn needle.

Pepperoni—Full Slice

With Chestnut Heather and G hook, ch 2.

Rnd 1 (RS): Work 6 sc in second ch from hook. Join with sl st to first sc, ch 1—6 sc.

Rnd 2: 2 sc in same sc as join and in each sc around. Join with sl st to first sc, ch 1—12 sc.

Rnd 3: Sc in same sc as join, 2 sc in next sc, [sc in next sc, 2 sc in next sc] five times. Join with sl st to first sc—18 sc.

Pepperoni—Half Slice

With Chestnut Heather and G hook, ch 2.

Row 1 (RS): Work 3 sc in second ch from hook. Ch 1, turn—3 sc.

Row 2: 2 sc in first sc and in each sc across. Ch 1, turn—6 sc.

Row 3: Sc in first sc, 2 sc in next sc, [sc in next sc, 2 sc in next sc] two times—9 sc.

Fasten off, leaving a long tail for sewing. Attach to the cheese along a straight edge of the pizza using the long tail and yarn needle.

 **Finishing:** Weave in ends.

A side salad is the perfect partner to a slice of pizza. And while this bowl happens to be filled with salad, it also makes a great container for strawberries, or just-picked green beans.

Side Salad Bowl

Ingredients

1 skein Lily Sugar n' Cream (cotton, 120 yds [109m] per 71g skein) in color White

1 skein Lily Sugar n' Cream (cotton, 120 yds [109m] per 71g skein) in color Hot Orange

1 skein Patons Classic Wool (wool, 223 yds [203m] per 100g skein) in color Bright Red

1 skein Patons Classic Wool (wool, 223 yds [203m] per 100g skein) in color Leaf Green

1 skein Patons Classic Wool (wool, 223 yds [203m] per 100g skein) in color Winter White

1 skein Yarn Source Sol (wool, 220 yds [200m] per 100g skein) in color Chartreuse

(or comparable worsted weight yarns)

US G / 4.0mm hook

US F / 3.75mm hook

yarn needle

Bowl

With White cotton and G hook, ch 2.

Rnd 1 (RS): Work 7 sc in second ch from hook. Join with sl st to first sc, ch 1—7 sc.

Rnd 2: Work 2 sc in same st as join and in next six sc. Join with sl st to first sc, ch 1—14 sc.

Rnd 3: Sc same st as join, 2 sc in next sc, [sc in next sc, 2 sc in next sc] six times. Join with sl st to first sc, ch 1—21 sc.

Rnd 4: Sc in same st as join and in next sc, 2 sc in next sc, [sc in each of the next two sc, 2 sc in next sc] six times. Join with sl st to first sc, ch 1—28 sc.

Rnd 5: Sl st in same st as join and in the next twenty-seven sc. Join with sl st to first sc, ch 1—28 sl sts.

Rnd 6: Working around the posts of the stitches in Rnd 4, work FP sc in first st and in each of the next twenty-seven sts. Join with sl st to first sc. Ch 1, turn —28 FP sc.

Rnd 7: Sc in same st as join and in each of the next two sc, 2 sc in next sc, [sc in each of the next three sts, 2 sc in next sc] six times. Join with sl st to first sc. Ch 1, turn—35 sc.

Rnd 8: Sc in same st as join and in each of the next three sc, 2 sc in next sc, [sc in each of the next four sc, 2 sc in next sc] six times. Join with sl st to first sc. Ch 1, turn—42 sc.

Rnd 9: Sc in same st as join and in the next 41 sc. Join with sl st to first sc. Ch 1, turn.

Rnd 10: Sc in same st as join and in each of the next four sc, 2 sc in next sc, [sc in each of the next five sc, 2 sc in next sc] six times. Join with sl st to first sc. Ch 1, turn—49 sc.

Rnd 11: Sc in same st as join and in the next forty-eight sc. Join with sl st to first sc. Ch 1, turn—48 sc.

Rnds 12–14: Rep Rnd 11. Change to Hot Orange yarn before the ch 1 at the end of Rnd 14.

Rnd 15: Sc in same st as join and in each of the next five sc, 2 sc in next st, [sc in each of the next six sc, 2 sc in next sc] six times. Join with sl st to first sc. Ch 1, turn—56 sc.

Rnd 16: Sc in same st as join and in the next fifty-five sc. Join with sl st to first sc—56 sc.

Fasten off, weave in ends.

Salad Leaves

Make three leaves in Chartreuse and three leaves in Leaf Green, with a mix of small and large leaves as desired.

Large Leaves

With G hook, ch 7.

Rnd 1 (RS): Work 3 hdc in second ch from hook, 3 dc in each of the next two ch, 3 hdc in next ch, 3 sc each of the next two ch, ch 1, continue around to the other side, working in free loops as follows: 3 hdc in first free loop, 3 dc in each of the next two free loops, 3 hdc in next loop, 3 sc each of the next two free loops. Join with sl st to the first hdc, ch 2—36 sts.

Rnd 2: Work 4 dc in each of the first four sts, sc in each of the next four sts, 4 dc in each of the next four sts, sc in the next twenty four sts. Join with sl st to first dc—60 sts.

Fasten off, weave in ends.

Small leaves

With G hook, ch 4.

Rnd 1 (RS): Work 3 dc in second ch from hook and in each ch to end. Continue around to the other side, working 3 dc in each free loop. Join with sl st to first dc, ch 1—18 dc.

Rnd 2: Work 4 sc in each of the first two sts, 4 dc in each of the next two sts, sc in each of the next nine sts, 4 dc in each of the next five sts. Join with sl st to first sc—45 sts.

Fasten off, weave in ends.

Onion

Make two:

With Winter White wool and F hook, ch 10.

Row 1 (RS): Sl st in second ch from hook and each ch to the end—9 sl sts.

Fasten off, weave in ends.

Tomato

Work as for Tomato in the Falafel Pita Pocket (page 59).

 **Finishing:** Assemble salad in bowl.

Every night can be taco night with a fun crocheted taco! Some tasty taco meat, cheese, lettuce and tomato all stack up in a corn tortilla for a South of the Border fiesta! Older kids will have a blast taking their taco apart and reassembling it, but for the younger set who still insists on eating their toys, I recommend stitching the pieces together securely for safety's sake.

Taco

Ingredients

1 skein Lion Brand Cotton-Ease (cotton/acrylic blend, 207 yds [188m] per 100g skein) in color Maize

1 skein Lion Brand Lion Wool (wool, 158 yds [144m] per 85g skein) in color Cocoa

1 skein Patons Classic Wool (wool, 223 yds [203m] per 100g skein) in color Leaf Green

1 skein Patons Classic Wool (wool, 223 yds [203m] per 100g skein) in color Bright Red

1 skein Lion Brand Lion Wool (wool, 158 yds [144m] per 85g skein) in color Goldenrod

(or comparable worsted weight yarns)

US G / 4.0mm hook

US F / 3.75mm hook

yarn needle

Taco Shell

With Maize cotton and G hook, ch 2.

Rnd 1 (RS): Work 6 sc in second ch from hook. Join with sl st to first sc, ch 1—6 sc.

Rnd 2: Work 2 sc in same st as join and in next five sc. Join with sl st to first sc, ch 1—12 sc.

Rnd 3: Sc in same st as join, work 2 sc in next sc, [sc in next sc, 2 sc in next sc] five times. Join with sl st to first sc, ch 1—18 sc.

Rnd 4: Sc in same st as join and in next sc, work 2 sc in next sc, [sc in each of the next two sc, 2 sc in next sc] five times. Join with sl st to first sc, ch 1—24 sc.

Rnd 5: Sc in same st as join and in each of the next two sc, work 2 sc in next sc, [sc in each of the next three sc, 2 sc in next sc] five times. Join with sl st to first sc, ch 1—30 sc.

Rnd 6: Sc in same st as join and in each of the next three sc, work 2 sc in next sc, [sc in each of the next four sc, 2 sc in next sc] five times. Join with sl st to first sc, ch 1—36 sc.

Rnd 7: Sc in same st as join and in each of the next four sc, work 2 sc in next sc, [sc in each of the next five sc, 2 sc in next sc] five times. Join with sl st to first sc, ch 1—42 sc.

Rnd 8: Sc in same st as join and in each of the next five sc, work 2 sc in next sc, [sc in each of the next six sc, 2 sc in next sc] five times. Join with sl st to first sc, ch 1—48 sc.

Rnd 9: Sc in same st as join and in each of the next six sc, work 2 sc in next sc, [sc in each of the next seven sc, 2 sc in next sc] five times. Join with sl st to first sc, ch 1—54 sc.

Rnd 10: Sc in same st as join and in each of the next seven sc, work 2 sc in next sc, [sc in each of the next eight sc, 2 sc in next sc] five times. Join with sl st to first sc, ch 1—60 sc.

Rnd 11: Sc in same st as join and in each of the next fifty-nine sc.

Fasten off, weave in ends.

Taco Meat

Make two:

With Cocoa and F hook, ch 5.

Row 1 (RS): Sc in second ch from hook, dc, sc, dc. Ch 1, turn—4 sts.

Row 2: Sc in first st, dc, sc, dc. Ch 1, turn.

Row 3: Rep Row 2.

Row 4: Work 2 sc in first st, dc, sc, dc. Ch 1, turn—5 sts.

Row 5: Sc in first st, dc, sc, dc in each of last two sts. Ch 1, turn.

Row 6: (Sc, dc) in first st, sc, dc, sc, dc. Ch 1, turn—6 sts.

Row 7: Sc in first st, dc, sc, dc dec over next two sts, skip last st. Ch 1, turn—4 sts.

Row 8: Sc in first st, dc, sc, dc. Ch 1, turn.

Row 9: Work 2 sc in first st, dc, sc, dc. Ch 1, turn—5 sts.

Row 10: Sc in first st, dc, sc, dc in each of last two sts. Ch 1, turn.

Row 11: (Sc, dc) in first st, sc, dc, sc, dc. Ch 1, turn—6 sts.

Row 12: Sc in first st, dc, sc, dc dec over next two sts, skip last st. Ch 1, turn—4 sts.

Row 13: Sc in first st, dc, sc, dc. Ch 1, turn.

Rows 14–17: Rep Row 13.

Match up the two pieces, and using Cocoa and F hook, sl st around the piece to secure. In between the sl sts, randomly add a picot (or two right next to each other) for added texture. Fasten off, weave in ends.

Using Goldenrod and yarn needle, randomly stitch yellow "cheese" all over the meat.

Lettuce

Make six:

With Leaf Green and F hook, ch 7.

Row 1 (RS): Work 3 hdc in second ch from hook, 3 dc in each of the next two ch, 3 hdc in next ch, 3 sc in each of the last two ch—18 sts.

Fasten off, weave in ends.

Tomato

Make six:

With Bright Red and F hook, ch 3.

Row 1 (RS): Sc in second ch from hook and in last ch. Ch 1, turn—2 sc.

Row 2: Sc in both sc. Ch 1, turn.

Rows 3–4: Rep Row 2.

Fasten off, leaving a long tail for sewing. Using long tail and yarn needle, sew one tomato piece to each lettuce piece. Weave in ends.

 **Finishing:** Place meat, lettuce and tomato in taco shell and enjoy!

Dessert

Some children will only eat that last bite of peas if there is the promise of dessert. Some adults, too! However old you are, dessert is like a little gift at the end of the day. I love the thought of a big Chocolate Cake Slice at the end of the day, or rounding off a day outside with a cool Ice Cream Sandwich. Even a bit of healthy fruit like a Pear or Strawberries is something special when it's at the end of a delicious dinner.

A cake leaves lots of room for creativity. Have fun with this recipe . . . make it a white or yellow cake instead of chocolate, or use bright blue yarn for the frosting.

Chocolate Cake Slice

Ingredients

1 skein Patons Classic Wool (wool, 223 yds [203m] per 100g skein) in color Winter White

1 skein Lion Brand Lion Wool (wool, 158 yds [144m] per 85g skein) in color Cocoa

(or comparable worsted weight yarns)

US G / 4.0mm hook

yarn needle

polyester fiberfill for stuffing

Special Stitches:

Triple Bobble (TRbobble)

*YO two times, insert hook into desired stitch and pull up a loop, [YO and pull through two loops] two times; rep from * four more times—six loops left on hook. YO and pull through all six loops. Sl st in same st—1 TRbobble created.

Bottom of cake slice

With Cocoa, ch 2.

Row 1 (RS): Sc in second ch from hook. Ch 1, turn—1 sc.

Row 2: Work 2 sc in sc. Ch 1, turn—2 sc.

Row 3: Sc in each sc. Ch 1, turn.

Row 4: Work 2 sc in first sc and in next sc. Ch 1, turn—4 sc.

Row 5: Sc in first sc and in each sc across. Ch 1, turn.

Row 6: Work 2 sc in first sc, sc in each of the next two sc, 2 sc in last sc. Ch 1, turn—6 sc.

Row 7: Sc in first sc and in each sc across. Ch 1, turn.

Row 8: Rep Row 7.

Row 9: Work 2 sc in first sc, sc in each of the next four sc, 2 sc in last sc. Ch 1, turn—8 sc.

Row 10: Sc in first sc and in each sc across. Ch 1, turn.

Row 11: Work 2 sc in first sc, sc in each of the next six sc, 2 sc in last sc. Ch 1, turn—10 sc.

Row 12: Sc in first sc and in each sc across. Ch 1, turn.

Row 13: Rep Row 12.

Row 14: Work 2 sc in first sc, sc in each of the next eight sc, 2 sc in last sc. Ch 1, turn—12 sc.

Row 15: Sc in first sc and in each sc across. Ch 1, turn.

Row 16: Work 2 sc in first sc, sc in each of the next ten sc, 2 sc in last sc. Ch 1, turn—14 sc.

Row 17: Sc in first sc and in each sc across. Ch 1, turn.

Row 18: Rep Row 17.

Row 19: Work 2 sc in first sc, sc in each of the next twelve sc, 2 sc in last sc. Ch 1, turn—16 sc.

Row 20: Sc in first sc and in each sc across. Ch 1, turn.

Row 21: Work 2 sc in first sc, sc in each of the next fourteen sc, 2 sc in last sc. Ch 1, turn—18 sc.

Row 22: Sc in first sc and in each sc across.

Row 23: Work 3 sc in first sc, sc across to last sc, work 3 sc in last sc, continue on around the side of the piece, working 1 sc in the end of each row down to the tip. Work 2 sc in the tip of the piece, then continue back up the side, once again working one sc in the end of each row. Join with sl st to the first sc.

Fasten off, weave in ends. Block flat.

Icing

With Winter White, work Rows 1–22 as for Cake Bottom.

Row 23 (RS): Sc in the first sc and in each sc across. Ch 1, turn—18 sc.

Row 24: Working in back loop only, sc in first sc and in each sc across. Ch 1, turn.

Row 25: Working through both loops, sc in first sc and in each sc across. Ch 1, turn.

Rows 26–34: Rep Row 25.

Row 35 (RS): Work 3 sc in first sc, sc across to last sc, work 3 sc in last sc, continue on around the side of the piece, working 1 sc in the end of each row down to the tip. Work 2 sc in the tip of the piece, then continue back up the side, once again working one sc in the end of each row. Join with sl st to the first sc.

Fasten off, weave in ends. Block flat.

Sides of cake slice

Make two:

With Cocoa, ch 24.

Row 1 (WS): Sc in second ch from hook and in each ch across. Ch 1, turn—23 sc.

Row 2: Sc in first sc and in each sc to end. Ch 1, turn.

Rows 3–5: Rep Row 2, changing to Winter White before the ch 1 at the end of Row 5.

Row 6: Now using Winter White, sc in first sc and in each sc across. Ch 1, turn.

Row 7: Sc in first sc and each sc across. Change to Cocoa. Ch 1, turn.

Row 8: Now using Cocoa, sc in first sc and in each sc across. Ch 1, turn.

Row 9–12: Rep Row 8, omitting the ch 1 at the end of Row 12.

Fasten off, weave in ends. Block flat.

Icing Piping

With Winter White, ch 15.

Row 1 (RS): Sc in second ch from hook and in each ch across. Ch 1, turn—14 sc.

Row 2: Sc in first sc, TRbobble in next sc, [sc in next sc, TRbobble in next sc] six times—7 sc and 7 TRbobbles.

Fasten off, leaving a long tail for sewing.

 Finishing: Lay the icing (top and back of the cake slice) down on a flat surface with WS facing up. Now lay the bottom of the cake slice down with WS facing up. Match up the straight edges of the two pieces. Using a long strand of Cocoa, sew through both loops of the sts in the straight edge of the bottom piece and through the top loop of the straight edge of the top and back piece to attach tog. Sew all of the way across. Fasten off, weave in ends.

Leave the attached pieces on the flat surface with RS down. Now take the two side pieces of the cake and lay them on the flat surface with RS down, one on each side of the assembled pieces. Line up the short side of the side pieces with the straight sides of the middle pieces. Using a long strand of Cocoa, sew through the ends of the rows of the side pieces and through the top loops of the sts along the straight edge of the other piece to secure. Do this on both sides.

Next, line up the sts of the long edge of the side pieces and the sts on the top icing piece. Sew through both loops of the side pieces and the back loop of the top piece to secure. Then, with WS of the cake facing, stitch the edges of the two side pieces tog to form the tip of the slice of cake. At this point, all seams should be sewn and closed, save for the bottom of the cake. Working through the front loop of the bottom and both loops of the sides, sew across to secure. Before piece is completely closed, stuff with polyester fiberfill.

 Finishing: To attach the piping to the cake, locate the edge of the cake where the top and back meet. Secure the piping piece on this edge by sewing across using Winter White. Fasten off, weave in ends.

 Imagine all of the varieties of cake you can whip up by varying cake color as well as frosting color. You could even create rainbow chips with tiny stitches.

Who can resist a warm, gooey chocolate chip cookie right out of the oven? These chocolate chip cookies are especially irresistible because they're fat free! For possible variations, make a cookie with extra chocolate chips, add dark chocolate (dark brown yarn), or macadamia nuts (ivory yarn).

Chocolate Chip Cookie

Ingredients

1 skein Patons Classic Wool (wool, 223 yds [203m] per 100g skein) in color Camel

1 skein Lion Brand Lion Wool (wool, 158 yds [144m] per 85g skein) in color Cocoa

(or comparable worsted weight yarns)

US G / 4.0mm hook

yarn needle

Make two:

With Camel, ch 2.

Rnd 1 (RS): Work 7 sc in second ch from hook. Join with sl st to first sc—7 sc.

Rnd 2: Ch 1. Work 2 sc in same st as join and in each of the next five sc. Join with sl st to first sc—14 sc.

Rnd 3: Ch 1. Sc in same sc as join, 2 sc in next sc, [sc in next sc, two sc in next sc] six times. Join with sl st to first sc—21 sc.

Rnd 4: Ch 1. Sc in same sc as join, sc in next sc, 2 sc in next sc, [sc in each of the next two sc, two sc in next sc] six times. Join with sl st to first sc—28 sc.

Rnd 5: Ch 1. Sc in same sc as join, sc in each of the next two sc, 2 sc in next sc, [sc in each of the next three sc, two sc in next sc] six times. Join with sl st to first sc—35 sc.

Fasten off and weave in ends.

❋ Finishing: Pin the two circles together with the right sides facing out. Using Camel and G hook, sc all the way around, working through both pieces.

Fasten off and weave in ends.

Chips

To make the chocolate chips, use a long strand of Cocoa and a yarn needle. Backstitch three to four times in one spot to create a raised area resembling a chocolate chip. Then run your yarn in between the two layers of the cookie to another spot and create another chocolate chip. Do this several times until you have a bunch of chocolate chips on the cookie.

Block flat.

Whoever came up with the idea for a dessert pizza must be a genius! It's such an ingenius treat—cookie crust covered with frosting and fresh fruit. Dessert doesn't get much better than this in my book.

Dessert Pizza

Ingredients

1 skein Patons Classic Wool (wool, 223 yds [203m] per 100g skein) in color Winter White

1 skein Patons Classic Wool (wool, 223 yds [203m] per 100g skein) in color Camel

1 skein Lion Brand Lion Wool (wool, 158 yds [144m] per 85g skein) in color Cocoa

1 skein Patons Classic Wool (wool, 223 yds [203m] per 100g skein) in color Bright Red

1 skein Patons Classic Wool (wool, 223 yds [203m] per 100g skein) in color Leaf Green

1 skein Patons Classic Wool (wool, 223 yds [203m] per 100g skein) in color Black

1 skein Lion Brand Fisherman's Wool (wool, 465 yds [425m] per 227g skein) in color Natural

(or comparable worsted weight yarns)

US G / 4.0mm hook

US F/ 3.75mm hook

stitch markers

yarn needle

Crust

Work as for Pizza. (page 87)

Chocolate Sauce

Work as for Pizza Sauce (page 89) using Cocoa.

Cream Cheese Frosting

Work as for Pizza Cheese (page 89) using Winter White.

Toppings

Kiwi Slice

With Natural and G hook, ch 2.

Rnd 1 (RS): Work 6 sc in second ch from hook. Join with sl st to first sc. Change to Leaf Green and ch 1—6 sc.

Rnd 2: Work 2 sc in same st as join and in next five sc. Join with sl st to first sc, ch 1—10 sc.

Rnd 3: Sc in same st as join and each sc around. Join with sl st to first sc.

Fasten off, leaving a long tail for sewing.

With a long strand of Black, stitch seeds around the edge of the white center round. Attach the slice to the pizza using the long tail.

Strawberry Slice

With White and F hook, ch 2.

Rnd 1 (RS): Work 5 sc in second ch from hook. Join with sl st to first sc. Change to Bright Red, ch 1—5 sc.

Rnd 2: Sc in same st as join, work 2 sc in each of the next four sc, sc in next sc. Join with sl st to first sc, ch 1—10 sc.

Row 3: Sc in same st as join and in next sc. Ch 1, turn—2 sc.

Row 4: Sc in same st as join and in next sc. Ch 1, turn—2 sc.

Row 5: Sc in same st as join and in next sc, continue to work sc around the whole piece, working one sc in each sc and one sc in the end of each row. Join with sl st to first sc—14 sc.

Fasten off, leaving a long tail for sewing. Use long tail to attach Strawberry Slice to pizza.

 **Finishing:** Weave in ends.

There's no sandwich as fun as an ice cream sandwich. Make it extra fun by using Paton's Classic Merino Wool in Petal Pink for strawberry ice cream, or Yarn Source Sol in Tan for chocolate.

Ice Cream Sandwich

Ingredients

1 skein Lion Brand Lion Wool (wool, 158 yds [144m] per 85g skein) in color Cocoa

1 skein Patons Classic Wool (wool, 223 yds [203m] per 100g skein) in color Winter White

(or comparable worsted weight yarns)

US G / 4.0mm hook

yarn needle

polyester fiberfill for stuffing

Cookie

Make two:

With Cocoa, ch 18.

Row 1 (RS): Sc in second ch from hook and in each ch across. Ch 1, turn—17 sc.

Row 2: Sc in first sc and in each sc across. Ch 1, turn.

Rows 3–10: Rep Row 2.

Row 11: Work 3 sc in first sc, sc in each of the next 15 sc, work 3 sc in next sc, continue around the side of the piece, working 1 sc in the end of each row, work 3 sc in corner, sc in each of the next fifteen free loops of the foundation ch, 3 sc in corner, continue up side working 1 sc in the end of each row. Join with sl st to first sc—60 sc.

Fasten off, weave in ends. Block flat.

Ice Cream

With the right side of one cookie facing you, join Winter White yarn in the back loop of any stitch.

Row 1: Working in BLO, sc in same st as join and in each of the next fifty-nine sc. Join with sl st to first sc. Ch 1. (60 sc)

Row 2: Working through both loops, sc in same st as join and in the next fifty-nine sc. Join with sl st to fisrt sc. Ch 1. (60 sc)

Rows 3–5: Repeat row 2, omitting the ch 1 at the end of row five.

Break off yarn, leaving a very long tail for sewing.

 Finishing: With RS facing out, line up the sts on the remaining cookie to the sts on the ice cream, pinning if necessary. Using the long tail left over from the ice cream, stitch through the back loops on the WS of the last row of the bottom piece. Do this all the way around the piece. Stuff lightly with polyester fiberfill before the ice cream sandwich is completely closed. Fasten off, weave in ends.

With RS of either the top or bottom of the sandwich facing, join Cocoa in the free loop of any stitch of the last row. Sc in that same st and in each st around. Join with a sl st to the first sc. Fasten off and weave in ends. Rep on the other side of the piece. This creates the 'lip' that sticks out from the ice cream.

Neopolitan Ice Cream Sandwich

Ingredients

1 skein Lion Brand Lion Wool (wool, 158 yds [144m] per 85g skein) in color Cocoa

1 skein Patons Classic Wool (wool, 223 yds [203m] per 100g skein) in color Winter White

1 skein Patons Classic Wool (wool, 223 yds [203m] per 100g skein) in color Petal Pink

1 skein Yarn Source Sol (wool, 220 yds [200m] per 100g skein) in color Tan

(or comparable worsted weight yarns)

US G / 4.0mm hook

yarn needle

polyester fiberfill for stuffing

Cookie

Make two:

Work as for Cookie (page 115).

Ice Cream

With RS of either cookie facing, count back 7 sts from the corner of the piece. Join Winter White in the back loop of that same st.

Rnd 1 (RS): Working in back loop only, sc in same st as join and in each of the next six sts. Change to Tan. Still working in back loop only, sc in each of the next twenty-three sts. Change to Winter White. Still working in back loop only, sc in each of the next seven sts. Change to Petal Pink. Still working in back loop only, sc in each of the next twenty-three sts. Join with sl st to first sc. Change to Winter White, ch 1—60 sc.

Rnd 2: Working through both loops now, sc in same sc as join and in next six sc. Change to Tan and sc in each of the next twenty-three sc. Change to Winter White and sc in each of the next seven sc. Change to Petal Pink and sc in each of the next twenty-three sc. Join with sl st to first sc. Change to Winter White. Ch 1—60 sc.

Rows 3–5: Rep Rnd 2, omitting the final change to Winter White and ch 1.

Fasten off, leaving a very long tail for sewing.

 Finishing: Assemble and finish as for Ice Cream Sandwich (page 116), using a long strand of Cocoa.

Change the nuts in this pattern to sprinkles, if you'd like, by using a variety of colors to backstitch on the surface of the chocolate. You could also mix things up by changing the flavor of the ice cream (Winter White) to Strawberry (Petal Pink).

Nutty Ice Cream Cone

Ingredients

1 skein Patons Classic Wool (wool, 223 yds [203m] per 100g skein) in color Camel

1 skein Patons Classic Wool (wool, 223 yds [203m] per 100g skein) in color Winter White

1 skein Lion Brand Lion Wool (wool, 158 yds [144m] per 85g skein) in color Cocoa

1 skein Lion Brand Cotton-Ease (cotton/acrylic blend, 207 yds [188m] per 100g skein) in color Maize

(or comparable worsted weight yarns)

US G / 4.0mm hook

stitch marker

yarn needle

polyester fiberfill for stuffing

 NOTES:

- This pattern is worked in continuous rnds. Please be sure to place a marker in the first stitch of rnd.

- Stuff with fiberfill as work progresses.

With Cocoa, ch 2.

Rnd 1: Work 8 sc in second ch from hook—8 sc

Rnd 2: Work 2 sc in first sc and in each sc around—16 sc.

Rnd 3: Sc in first sc, 2 sc in next sc, [sc in next sc, 2 sc in next sc] seven times—24 sc.

Rnd 4: Sc in first sc, sc in next sc, 2 sc in next sc, [sc in each of next two sc, 2 sc in next sc] seven times—32 sc.

Rnd 5: Sc in first sc and each of the next two sc, 2 sc in next sc, [sc in each of the next three sc, 2 sc in next sc] seven times—40 sc.

Rnd 6: Sc in first sc and each sc around.

Rnds 7–8: Rep Rnd 6.

Rnd 9: Sc in first sc and each of the next five sc, dec over next two sc, [sc in each of next six sc, dec over next two sc] four times—35 sc.

Rnd 10: Sc in first sc and each of the next four sc, dec over next two sc, [sc in each of the next five sc, dec over next two sc] four times—30 sc.

Rnd 11: Sc in first sc and each sc around.

Rnd 12: Rep Rnd 11.

Rnd 13: Sc in first sc and each of the next three sc, dec over next two sc, [sc in each of the next four sc, dec over next two sc] four times—25 sc.

Rnd 14: Sc in first sc and each sc around.

Change to Winter White.

Rnd 15: Working in back loop only, sc in first sc and each sc around.

Change to Camel.

Rnd 16: Working in back loop only, sc in first sc and each sc around.

Rnd 17: Sc in first sc and each of the next 22 sc, dec over last two sc—24 sc.

Rnd 18: Sc in first sc and each of the next five sc, dec over next two sc, [sc in each of the next six sc, dec over next two sc] two times—21 sc.

Rnd 19: Sc in first sc and in each sc around.

Rnd 20: Sc in first sc and in each of the next four sc, dec over next two sc, [sc in each of the next five sc, dec over next two sc] two times—18 sc.

Rnd 21: Sc in first sc and in each sc around.

Rnds 22–24: Rep Rnd 21.

Rnd 25: Sc in first sc and in each of the next three sc, dec over next two sc, [sc in each of the next four sc, dec over next two sc] two times—15 sc.

Rnd 26: Sc in first sc and in each sc around.

Rnds 27–28: Rep Rnd 26.

Rnd 29: Sc in first sc and in each of the next two sc, dec over next two sc, [sc in each of the next three sc, dec over next two sc] two times—12 sc.

Rnd 30: Sc in first sc and in each sc around.

Rnd 31: Sc in first sc and in next sc, dec over next two sc, [sc in each of the next two sc, dec over next two sc] two times—9 sc.

Rnd 32: Sc in first sc and in each sc around.

Rnd 33: Sc in first sc, dec over next two sc, [sc in next sc, dec over next two sc] two times—6 sc.

Rnd 34: Sc in first sc and in each sc around.

Fasten off, leaving a long tail for sewing. Using yarn needle, weave the tail through the remaining 6 sts and pull tight to close.

Nuts

Using yarn needle and a long strand of Maize yarn, backstitch two times in the same spot on the chocolate area of the ice cream cone. Do this randomly, as much or as little as you'd like, to create the nuts. Use several 24" (61cm) lengths of yarn, rather than one long strand, to prevent tangling.

 **Finishing:** Weave in ends.

If I could sing, I would find an orchard and serenade a pear. That might be a little embarrassing (for me and the pear), so I'll settle for crocheting an ode to my most favorite fruit.

Pear

Ingredients

1 skein Cascade 220 (wool, 220 yds [200m] per 100g skein) in color Pear

1 skein Patons Classic Wool (wool, 223 yds [203m] per 100g skein) in color Chestnut Brown

(or comparable worsted weight yarns)

US G / 4.0mm hook

yarn needle

stitch marker

polyester fiberfill for stuffing

 NOTES:

- This pattern is worked in continuous rnds. Please be sure to place a marker in the first stitch of rnd.

- Pear is worked from top down.

With Pear, ch 2.

Rnd 1 (RS): Work 6 sc in second ch from hook—6 sc.

Rnd 2: Work 2 sc in each sc around—12 sc.

Rnd 3: [Sc in the next sc, 2 sc in next sc] six times—18 sc.

Rnd 4: [Sc in each of the next two sc, 2 sc in next sc] six times—24 sc.

Rnd 5: [Sc in each of the next three sc, 2 sc in next sc] six times—30 sc.

Rnd 6: [Sc in each of the next four sc, 2 sc in next sc] six times—36 sc.

Rnd 7: [Sc in each of the next five sc, 2 sc in next sc] six times—42 sc.

Rnd 8: Sc in each sc around.

Rnds 9–11: Rep Rnd 8.

Rnd 12: [Sc in each of the next five sc, dec over next two sc] six times—36 sc.

Rnd 13: Sc in each sc around.

Rnd 14: [Sc in each of the next four sc, dec over next two sc] six times—30 sc.

Rnd 15: [Sc in each of the next three sc, dec over next two sc] six times—24 sc.

Rnd 16: Sc in each sc around.

Rnds 17–18: Rep Rnd 16.

Rnd 19: [Sc in each of the next two sc, dec over next two sc] six times—18 sc.

Rnd 20: Sc in each sc around.

Rnd 21: [Sc in next sc, dec over next two sc] six times—12 sc.

Rnd 22: Sc in each sc around.

Stuff with polyester fiberfill.

Rnd 23: [Dec over next two sc] six times—6 sc.

Fasten off, leaving a long end for sewing. With yarn needle, weave long end through last 6 sts, pull tight to close. Fasten off, weave in ends.

Stem

With Chestnut Brown, ch 6. Sl st in second ch from hook and in each ch across. Fasten off, leaving a long end for sewing. Attach to the top of the pear using long end and yarn needle.

 **Finishing:** Weave in ends.

Why save Pumpkin Pie for an autumnal occasion? I could eat this rich dessert any month of the year. Modify this pattern to make a simple cherry pie by using Bright Red yarn for the sides of the pie filling and Camel yarn for the top.

Pumpkin Pie

Ingredients

1 skein Lion Brand Lion Wool (wool, 158 yds [144m] per 85g skein) in color Pumpkin

1 skein Patons Classic Wool (wool, 223 yds [203m] per 100g skein) in color Camel

1 skein Patons Classic Wool (wool, 223 yds [203m] per 100g skein) in color Winter White

(or comparable worsted weight yarn)

US G / 4.0mm hook

stitch marker

yarn needle

polyester fiberfill for stuffing

Pie Crust

With Camel, ch 2.

Row 1 (RS): Work 2 sc in second ch from hook. Ch 1, turn—2 sc.

Row 2: Sc in each sc across. Ch 1, turn.

Row 3: Work 2 sc in first sc and in next sc. Ch 1, turn—4 sc.

Rows 4–5: Sc in each sc across. Ch 1, turn.

Row 6: Work 2 sc in first sc, sc in each of the next two sc, 2 sc in last sc. Ch 1, turn—6 sc.

Rows 7–8: Sc in each sc across. Ch 1, turn.

Row 9: Work 2 sc in first sc, sc in each of the next four sc, 2 sc in last sc. Ch 1, turn—8 sc.

Rows 10–11: Sc in each sc across. Ch 1, turn.

Row 12: Work 2 sc in first sc, sc in each of the next six sc, 2 sc in last sc. Ch 1, turn—10 sc.

Rows 13–14: Sc in each sc across. Ch 1, turn.

Row 15: Work 2 sc in first sc, sc in each of the next eight sc, 2 sc in last sc. Ch 1, turn—12 sc.

Rows 16–17: Sc in each sc across. Ch 1, turn.

Row 18: Work 2 sc in first sc, sc in each of the next ten sc, 2 sc in last sc. Ch 1, turn—14 sc.

Rows 19–20: Sc in each sc across. Ch 1, turn.

Row 21: Work 2 sc in first sc, sc in each of the next twelve sc, 2 sc in last sc. Ch 1, turn—16 sc.

Row 22: Sc in each sc across. Ch 1, turn.

Row 23: Working in back loop only, sc in each sc across. Ch 1, turn—20 sc.

Row 24: Working through both loops, sc in each sc across. Ch 1, turn.

Rows 25–31: Rep Row 24.

Row 32: Work 3 hdc in first sc, sl st in each of the next two sc, [3 hdc in next sc, sl st in each of the next two sc] across, ending with 3 hdc in last st.

Fasten off, weave in ends. Block flat.

Filling

Top

With Pumpkin, ch 2.

Work as for Pie Crust up to Row 21. Fasten off, weave in ends. Block flat.

Sides

With Pumpkin, ch 7.

Row 1 (RS): Sc in second ch from hook and in each ch across. Ch 1, turn—6 sc.

Row 2: Sc in first sc and in each sc across. Ch 1, turn.

Rows 3–22: Rep Row 2.

Row 23: Working in back loop only, sc in first sc and in each sc across. Ch 1, turn.

Row 24: Working through both loops, sc in first sc and in each sc across. Ch 1, turn.

Row 25–45: Rep Row 24.

Fasten off, weave in ends. Block flat.

 Finishing: On the side piece, Row 23 forms kind of a "hinge" in the piece. This hinge row matches up with the beginning tip of the pie crust. Using a long strand of Pumpkin and a yarn needle, join the hinge row (RS facing) to the tip of the pie crust. Whipstitch the two pieces tog down one side and up the bottom crust, and then up the side piece (take care to match up the sts or pie will be bunchy). Rep on the other side.

Place the Top Filling piece on top of the Side pieces and whipstitch tog. Stuff with polyester fiberfill before closing. Fasten off, weave in ends.

Whipped Cream

With Winter White, ch 31.

Row 1 (RS): Sc in second ch from hook and in each ch across—30 sc.

Fasten off, leaving a long tail for sewing.

Coil the piece around on itself, stitching to secure. While turning the piece, "stack" the chain up on top of the coil before it to form the different levels of the whipped cream.

Sew to the top of the pumpkin pie. Fasten off, weave in ends.

Strawberries are summer's gift to us; perfectly sweet little morsels of heaven, ready to top a cake or pie, or to be eaten on their own. A few of these would look so pretty on a plate with a slice of chocolate cake (page 103).

Strawberry

Ingredients

1 skein Patons Classic Wool (wool, 223 yds [203m] per 100g skein) in color Bright Red

1 skein Cascade 220 (wool, 220 yds [200m] per 100g skein) in color Palm

(or comparable worsted weight yarns)

US G / 4.0mm hook

stitch marker

yarn needle

polyester fiberfill for stuffing

 NOTE:

This pattern is worked in continuous rnds. Please be sure to place a marker in the first stitch of rnd.

Strawberry

With Bright Red, ch 2.

Rnd 1 (RS): Work 6 sc in second ch from hook—6 sc.

Rnd 2: [Sc in the next sc, 2 sc in next sc] three times—9 sc.

Rnd 3: [Sc in each of the next two sc, 2 sc in next sc] three times—12 sc.

Rnd 4: Sc in each sc around.

Rnd 5: [Sc in each of the next three sc, 2 sc in next sc] three times—15 sc.

Rnd 6: [Sc in each of the next four sc, 2 sc in next sc] three times—18 sc.

Rnd 7: Sc in each sc around.

Rnd 8: [Sc in each of the next five sc, 2 sc in next sc] three times—21 sc.

Rnd 9: [Sc in each of the next six sc, 2 sc in next sc] three times—24 sc.

Rnd 10: Sc in each sc around.

Rnd 11: [Dec over next two sc] twelve times—12 sc.

Rnd 12: [Dec over next two sc] six times—6 sc.

Stuff with fiberfill.

Fasten off, leaving a long end for sewing. With yarn needle, weave long end through last 6 sts, pull tight to close. Fasten off, weave in ends.

Stem

With Palm, ch 2.

Rnd 1 (RS): Work 6 sc in second ch from hook. Join with sl st to first sc.

Rnd 2: *Ch 3, sl st in second ch from hook and next ch, sl st in same st as ch 3*, sl st in next sc, rep from * to * two times in same sc, sl st in next sc, rep from * to * in same sc, sl st in next sc, rep from * to * two times in same sc, sl st in next sc, rep from * to * in same sc, sl st in next sc, rep from * to * two times in same sc. Fasten off, leaving a long tail for sewing.

 Finishing: Attach the green stem to the top of the strawberry using long tail and yarn needle. Fasten off, weave in ends.

There are relatively few techniques you must master in order to whip up the treats in this book. Even if you have never crocheted before, take a look at the basic techniques offered on these pages, and I hope you'll be stiching away something tasty in no time.

Basic Crochet

Abbreviations

[ ] *work instructions within brackets as many times as directed*

approx *approximately*

beg *begin/beginning*

BLO *back loop only*

ch *chain stitch*

dbch *double chain stitch*

dc *double crochet*

dec *decrease/ decreases/decreasing*

FLO *front loop only*

foll *follow/follows/ following*

FP *front post*

hdc *half double crochet*

lp(s) *loops*

oz *ounces*

p *picot*

rep *repeat*

RS *right side*

sc *single crochet*

sk *skip*

Sl st *slip sitich*

sp *space*

st(s) *stitch(es)*

tog *together*

tr *triple crochet*

WS *wrong side*

Pantry Staples

Crochet hooks:
Individual patterns call for specific sizes, but it's a good idea to keep several sizes on hand. I used primarily sizes US G (4.0mm) and US F (3.75mm) in this book.

Yarn needle:
You'll need at least one of these to weave in the tail ends of yarn as well as to stitch elements together, such as a leafy top to a carrot.

Stitch markers:
These help you keep your place at certain points in a pattern.

Scissors:
The easiest way to break your yarn is with a good pair of scissors.

Polyester fiberfill:
Some items call for this, such as a strawberry or a bagel half. Yarn or fabric scraps can be substituted.

Rust-proof straight pins:
These will help you hold elements in place as you stitch them together.

Holding the Hook and Yarn

Traditionally, the hook is held in the right hand and the yarn is held in the left hand. However, many crocheters find it easer to hold the hook and the yarn in their right hand and hold just the work and the working loop in their left.

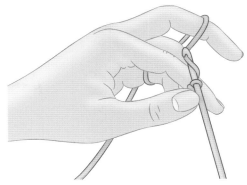

2. Grip the base of the starting slip knot underneath the hook and between the thumb and first finger of your left hand. Leave the cut end to dangle free and take the ball end over your fingers, wrapping it around your little finger.

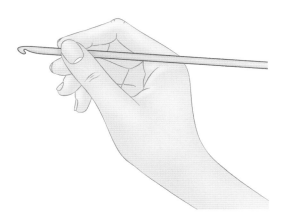

1. Hold the hook as you would a pen or a knitting needle.

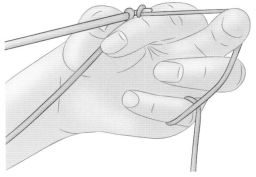

3. To begin each stitch, wrap the yarn around the hook by turning the hook clockwise around the yarn or by looping the yarn over the hook from the back to the front. Extend your middle finger to help regulate the tension of the yarn, taking care to not pull the yarn too tightly.

Slip Knot

This knot creates your first stitch and is the technique you will use to start any project.

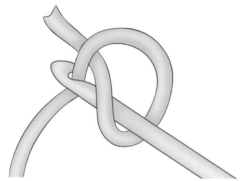

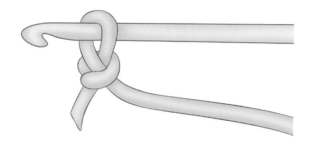

1. Leaving a short tail, create a loop near the end of the yarn. Insert a crochet hook through the loop and pick up the yarn that leads toward the ball or skein.

2. Pull the yarn through the loop and gently pull the yarn to tighten the new loop around the hook. This will now be your first stitch.

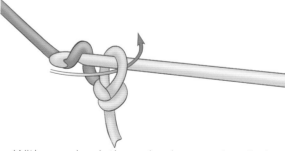

Chain (ch)

All of the projects in this book begin with a length of chain stitches and these also appear in the middle of patterns.

With your hook through a loop or the slip knot, wrap the yarn from the back, over the hook toward the front, and down again, so you have wrapped it completeley around the hook. Pull the yarn through the loop. Repeat for as many chain (ch) stitches as directed.

Single Crochet (sc)

All of the projects in this book begin with a length of chain stitches and these also appear in the middle of patterns.

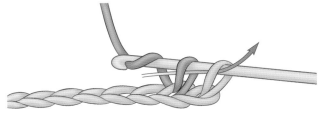

1. When directed, insert the hook into the work at the required loop. Wrap the yarn over the hook from back to front and pull the yarn through the loop on the hook. There should now be two loops on the hook.

2. Wrap the yarn over the hook again, and this time pull it through both loops on the hook. This completes one single crochet (sc) stitch.

Double Crochet (dc)

Unlike a single crochet stitch, which is short and compact, a double-crochet stitch is longer and will lengthen/add height to the work.

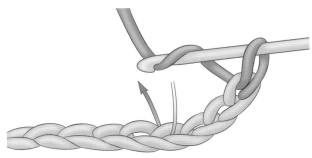

1. Wrap the yarn over the hook, but don't pull it through the loop on the hook yet. With the yarn around the hook, insert the hook into the work at the directed spot.

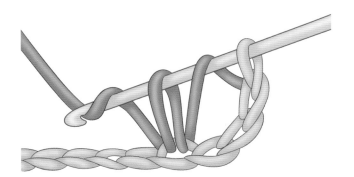

2. Wrap the yarn around the hook and pull the yarn through just the work. Now there are three loops on the hook. Wrap the yarn around the hook again and pull it through just the first two loops on the hook.

3. Wrap the yarn around the hook again and pull this through the new loops on the hook. This completes one double crochet (dc) stitch.

Half Double Crochet (hdc)

This is a variation of the double crochet stitch, and it results in a height that's between a single crochet and a double crochet.

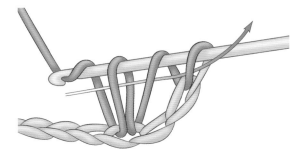

Repeat steps 1 and 2 for Double Crochet, but instead of pulling it through just the first two loops, pull it through all three. This completes the Half Double Crochet (hdc) stitch.

Triple Crochet (tr)

Another version of the double crochet stitch, this creates the tallest stitch of the three variations.

1. To begin this stitch, wrap the yarn around the hook twice before inserting it into the work.

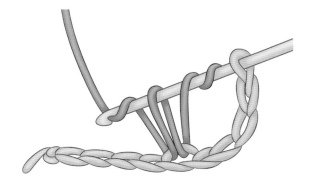

2. Wrap the yarn around the hook again and pull this new loop through the first two loops on the hook, leaving two loops remaining on the hook.

3. Wrap the yarn around the hook again and pull that loop through the work. Now there should be four loops on the hook. Wrap the yarn around the hook once more and pull that new loop through only the first two loops on the hook.

4. Wrap the yarn around the hook a final time and pull that loop through both remaining loops on the hook to complete the Triple Crochet stitch.

Slip Stitch (Sl st)

Just the opposite of the Double, Half Double and Triple Crochet stitches, this stitch adds virtually no height to the work and is typically used to move the hook and working loop to a new point, or to join pieces together.

Insert the hook into the work at the directed point. Bring the yarn over the hook and pull that loop through the work and the loop on the hook to complete the Slip Stitch.

Back Loop Only

By working the yarn through just one half (the back half) of the V formed by previous stitches, a horizontal bar across the work is created.

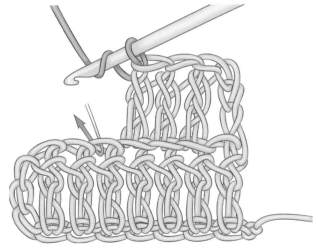

Slide the hook through the work between the two bars that form the V, picking up only the back half of the loop.

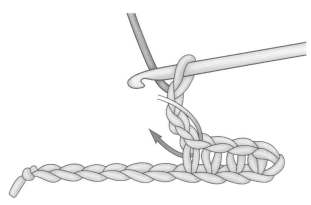

1. Work up to the point where you want the pico to be centered. Make the directed number of chain stitches (often this is three).

The stitch is completed by working a stitch into the top of the last stitch worked before the short chain. To work this stitch, twist the hook and insert it down through the top of the last "real" stitch worked.

2. The picot can be closed with either a Slip Stitch or with a Single Crochet. With a Slip Stitch, the ends of the small chain are kept tightly together, resulting in more pronounced bump. A Single Crochet increases the size of the ring somewhat, so the effect is a bit more subtle. Check the pattern to see what is called for.

Changing Colors

Because of the nature of crochet, the last loop of one stitch actually sits on top of the next stitch, creating two bars of yarn that form a complete V. This means that a color should be changed just before completing the last stitch of the old color.

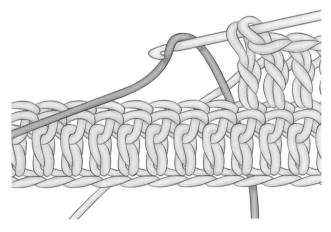

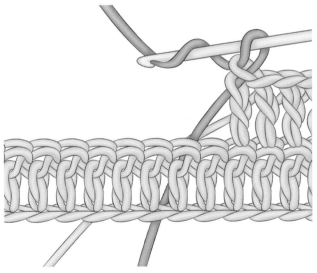

1. Work the last stitch of the old color up to the stage where the next step would be to wrap the yarn around the hook before drawing it through all loops on the hook. (For most stitches, this means stopping at the point when there are just two remaining loops on the hook.) Let the old yarn drop to the wrong side of the work and pick up the new yarn, leaving the tail on the wrong side as well.

2. Wrap the new yarn around the hook and complete the stitch using the new yarn.

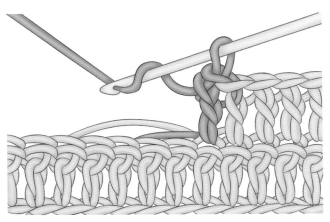

3. Continue the next stitches with the new yarn. The two remaining tails sitting on the wrong side of the work may be woven into the work using a yarn needle.

Overcast Stitch for Seaming

This method for seaming works to join most types of crochet. It isn't bulky and if done correctly, is practically invisible.

Note: If you leave a long tail when you start a piece of work, that tail can be used for seaming when you're done.

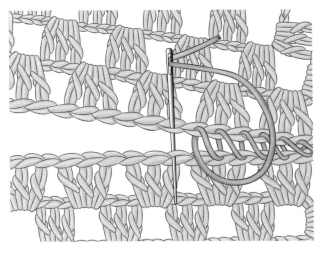

Lay the two edges to be joined alongside one another. Working along the edges, pick up one stitch at a time with the threaded needle. If you are joining two sides that are row-end edges, make stitches that are the same size as the ones across the crochet rows.

Resources

Yarn Source Sol yarn:
www.lambikins.com

Patons yarn:
www.patonsyarns.com

Lion Brand yarn:
www.lionbrand.com

Lamb's Pride Yarn:
www.brownsheep.com

Lily Sugar 'n Cream Yarn:
www.sugarncream.com

Index

Indulge Your Creative Side With These Other F+W Media Titles

Plush You!
Kristen Rask

This showcase of 100 plush toys, many with patterns and instructions, will inspire you to join in on the DIY toy phenomenon. Simple projects book provide instant gratification for beginners and new ideas and inspiration for experienced, full-time toymakers. Stuffed space creatures and lovable monsters, along with the occasional cut of beef and other squeezable subjects make this an irresistibly hip book that you just want to hug.

ISBN-10: 1-58180-996-4
ISBN-13: 978-1-58180-996-1
paperback with flaps
144 pages
Z0951

Warm Fuzzies
Betz White

Warm Fuzzies is filled with techniques, tips and patterns for creating 30 cute and colorful felted projects, including cozy pillows and throws as well as comfortable hats, scarves, pincushions and handbags. Author Betz White will show you how to felt thrift store and bargain sweaters, then cut them up and use them to make quick, adorable projects for the whole family.

ISBN-10: 1-60061-007-2
ISBN-13: 978-1-60061-007-3

paperback
144 pages
Z1026

Mr. Funky's Super Crochet Wonderful
Narumi Ogawa

Mr. Funky's Super Crochet Wonderful is filled with 25 supercute crochet patterns for adorable Japanese-style stuffed animals and accessories. You'll find candy-color elephants, panda bears, kitty cats, hamsters and even a snake, plus fashionable hats, armwarmers and purses for girls of all ages. Each pattern features written out instructions as well as traditional amigurumi, or Japanese crochet diagrams.

ISBN 10: 1-58180-966-2
ISBN 13: 978-1-58180-966-4
paperback
112 pages
Z0697

Crochet Squared
Marsha Polk

If you can crochet a simple scarf, you can make any of the stylish and sophisticated body wraps and accessories featured in *Crochet Squared*. Each of over 20 projects in the book is based on a simple square or rectangle shape, allowing even beginning crocheters to make gorgeous works of art. And don't worry—just because these projects are built around the square doesn't mean you'll look like one wearing them! You'll also find a practical guide to basic crochet techniques.

ISBN-10: 1-58180-833-X
ISBN-13: 978-1-58180-833-9
paperback
128 pages
33507

These books and other fine North Light titles are available at your local craft retailer, bookstore or online supplier, or visit us at www.mycraftivity.com.